lo

Cover:
A color variety of the Peach-faced Lovebird. Photo by Harry V. Lacey.

Frontispiece:
Agapornis roseicollis, the Peach-faced Lovebird. Photo by Mueller-Schmida.

Photos by Miceli Studios were made with the cooperation of Novak's Aviaries, Deer Park, New York.

ISBN 0-87666-957-7

Based on *Foreign Birds for Cage and Aviary.*

Distributed in the U.S.A. by T.F.H. Publications, Inc., 211 West Sylvania Avenue, P.O. Box 27, Neptune City, N.J. 07753; in England by T.F.H. (Gt. Britain) Ltd., 13 Nutley Lane, Reigate, Surrey; in Canada to the book store and library trade by Clarke, Irwin & Company, Clarwin House, 791 St. Clair Avenue West, Toronto 10, Ontario; in Canada to the pet trade by Rolf C. Hagen Ltd., 3225 Sartelon Street, Montreal 382, Quebec; in Southeast Asia by Y.W. Ong, 9 Lorong 36 Geylang, Singapore 14; in Australia and the south Pacific by Pet Imports Pty. Ltd., P.O. Box 149, Brookvale 2100, N.S.W., Australia. Published by T.F.H. Publications, Inc. Ltd., The British Crown Colony of Hong Kong.

Contents

Preface

Interest in the rarer forms of cagebirds has received a helpful nudge in recent years by extremely restrictive regulations by federal and state governments. Contrary to predictions, there has been an impressive increase in the number of fanciers and in the number of entries in bird shows. There also has been—as both cause and effect—an increase in bird prices.

After having been banned entirely from importation for nearly half a century, psittacine birds again became admissible into the United States after the government discovered that chlortetracycline treatment reduced the threat from ornithosis (erroneously called "parrot fever"). Existing stocks of psittacine birds received an infusion of fresh blood, and fanciers were able to expand their collections with wild and domestic specimens from abroad.

But shortly after psittacines again became eligible for importation, the world-wide epidemic of Exotic Newcastle Disease struck, and the ports were slammed shut tighter than ever was done for smallpox or the plague. No feathered creature entered the country legally for three years.

Such action was predicted to prove fatal for the cagebird fancy, but it was a boon instead. Suddenly the rarer species became more desirable, and today demand continues to outstrip the supply. This is especially true of lovebirds.

There are ten lovebird species, but by far the most common in the United States today is the Peach-faced. One reason for its popularity is the various mutations that have appeared: pied in various colors, blue, yellow ("cherry-head"), white (silver), lutino, albino, and cinnamon. When all of these colors are common enough to appear in numbers, the lovebird benches in bird shows will rival the budgie divisions for color.

And we can expect this to happen. Lovebirds have a great appeal. They are gorgeous things to look at, each species with a different kind of beauty. They are small enough to be quartered in limited space. The species kept by beginners breed quite easily. They are not given to illness. New mutations make it exciting for those who crave rare color forms. And some of the species are extremely difficult to find and are even more challenging to breed.

In the lovebird fancy there is something for everyone, novice or seasoned veteran, rich or poor, rancher or apartment-dweller. Everyone who has room in his heart for a colorful and lively companion can accommodate a lovebird. As an individual pet, a lovebird is an irresistible member of the family and quickly becomes indispensable. Most fanciers, however, will be keeping them in breeding pairs.

There is a genuine satisfaction in bringing a pair of love-birds into breeding condition, watching the hen tuck nesting material into her feathers to transport it to the nest, waiting impatiently during the incubation period, hearing the first faint squeaks of new life, watching the chicks double their size each time the nestbox is opened, finally emerging as only slightly subdued copies of their parents. Here is the ultimate thrill for the person who acquires a pair for breeding.

Part of the satisfaction of owning lovebirds is in meeting others who also enjoy lovebirds. Most states have cagebird clubs that meet monthly. There is a national specialist society that publishes a monthly bulletin containing helpful articles: The African Love Bird Society, Box 142, San Marcos, CA 92069. Membership can be very productive.

Mr. Soderberg has written this book to provide a guide for lovebird fanciers, both beginning and advanced. It should help every reader find more enjoyment in his love-birds and, I hope, success in the fancy.

Val Clear

Anderson, Indiana
August, 1977

1: Accommodation

Anyone who becomes interested in lovebirds and finally makes up his mind to keep them, should first sit down and consider very carefully the question of accommodation, for unless this problem has been thought out with great care, the bird-keeper will probably experience disappointment quite early in his career as an aviculturalist.

Many who have made a start with bird-keeping have given up the hobby in despair merely because they failed to think about the most important things first, in this case the cage or aviary in which the birds were to be housed.

BASIC PRINCIPLES

There are certain basic principles in the housing of lovebirds which just cannot be ignored. Most animals, whether they are birds or fur-bearing creatures, must have the right type of environment if they are to survive for any length of time in captivity. There is also a moral obligation, and they must be provided with comfortable quarters if they are to be happy under the unnatural conditions which they are bound to experience when they are kept as domestic pets.

The requirements of lovebirds are comparatively easy to fulfil, and there can be no excuse for neglecting any of them.

In a state of nature most birds are accustomed to fly, and, apart from the breeding season when the hen has to spend a good deal of her time more or less immobile on the nest, much of their time is spent on the wing even if it is only a matter of flitting from perch to perch. Thus, the area in which they are confined becomes a matter of considerable importance.

Birds should not be kept in cages in which they have no opportunity to exercise their wings. It is also essential that they should not only be able to flap their wings at will, but further, that they should be able to use them in actual flight. This must mean that there is an absolute minimum to the length of the cage from perch to perch. Now it is quite possible to keep birds for long periods in reasonable health in a small cage of no greater length than 24 in., but generally speaking, these small cages should only be used for birds which for many generations have been bred in captivity and have been bred in similar cages, such as Canaries, Bengalese Finches, or Zebra Finches.

Most of the lovebirds now available in this country are the result of many generations of cage aviculture and they are more adaptable to cages than would have been true some years ago. Nevertheless, the fancier will have greater success with breeding pairs if the cage is as large as possible. Breeding pairs get quite pugnacious and if kept in an aviary, one pair can monopolize a sizeable space. It is more practical in most cases to keep breeders in cages, and if possible these should have a long dimension of at least thirty six-inches.

CAGE TYPES AND FITTINGS

There are two main types of cage, and these are essentially different, but between these two extremes there can be, and often are, a number of modified patterns.

First of all, there is the cage made entirely of wire, which has been popular for very many years. The design of many of these cages is extremely decorative, and they are painted in gay colors to make them even more pleasing to the eye. Now there is no reason to condemn a cage of this sort out of hand, but few will disagree that this is a cage with very definite limitations. In the first place, quite apart from the point of view of appearance, there is no real value in having a cage of complicated design merely because it looks more attractive to the eye. Wire cages which are simple in line have a good deal to recommend them when that is the type of cage that is felt desirable. Usually they are rather on the small side, although many different sizes can be made to order. For most lovebirds this small wire cage may have little to recommend it, but the fact remains that it is still popular.

Simplicity of design can be a valuable feature in an all-wire cage, and the size of the cage plays a very important role in determining its suitability for housing lovebirds. The spaces between the bars should not be large enough to permit escape but also must not be so small that they restrict viewing. Photo courtesy Prevue Metal Products.

One of the arguments put forward for the use of the all-wire cage is simplicity of cleaning, but if this task is to be really simple, there should be no fancy work attached to the cage at all. The more the decoration and ornamentation the more difficult it is really to get down to the task of a thorough cleaning.

One very serious disadvantage with the all-wire cage is that it affords little protection to the bird from draughts which can be, and often are, fatal. Thus, if you decide that your lovebirds are to be kept in a wire cage, then you must

There are very many good cages available for purchase at pet stores, but some are designed for birds other than lovebirds; inexperienced bird-keepers are well advised to seek the advice of knowledgeable sellers of pet supplies before buying a home for their lovebirds. The choice of cage design will depend to some extent on the amount of money the buyer can afford to spend and the space available for housing the cage.

also pay great attention to the situation of the cage in the room, which will usually be the living-room of the family. To hang it between a door and a window is to put it in the very spot in which draughts are inevitable. There are, in fact, many rooms in which it is quite impossible to put a wire cage so that it will be free from all draught. If you should decide that the only place for it is on a wall, then you have lost much of the apparent virtue of an all-wire cage, for you have actually provided it with a solid back.

Another point to bear in mind with cages of this type is that the bird is exposed on all sides, and there is really no place in which it can find seclusion. If people approach it from both sides and it is a timid bird, the possibility is that it will panic. However, there are many people who still believe in a cage of this type, and, always provided that they bear in mind its defects and the necessary precautions which have to be taken to protect the birds, there can be no justification for condemning such a cage absolutely. But sooner or later it is likely to be replaced with a box cage if the owner is interested in breeding the birds rather than having them merely as family pets.

Lovebirds are less easy to breed than some of the more popular psittacine species like budgies, but it is possible to breed them without constructing an aviary and going into bird-breeding on a large basis. Here a lovebird cage is shown with a nesting box attached to its rear; this is the most economical arrangement for breeding lovebirds without purchase or construction of a breeding unit separate from the regular housing unit. Photo by Miceli Studios.

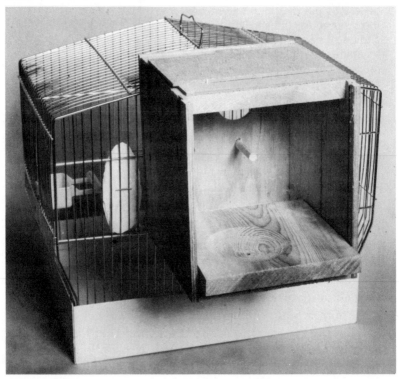

The box-type cage differs from the all-wire page primarily in having three of its sides enclosed, with only one side left free for viewing.

THE BOX-TYPE CAGE

This is a very simple cage in which the sides, top and back are solid. Several inches at the bottom of the front are also solid, while the rest is made up of metal cross-bars through which other vertical wires pass and are soldered so that the whole thing remains firm. Whether such a cage is made of wood, metal or some other substitute material is usually not of very great importance, with perhaps one qualification. If the cage is made entirely of metal, it should not be used in a situation where the temperature can fall to a

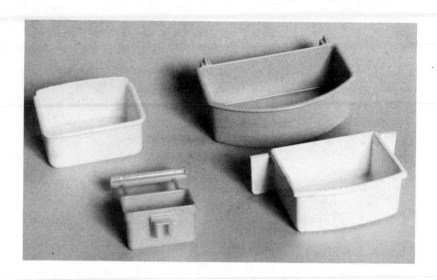

Handy and inexpensive bird accessories like feed and water containers, beak conditioners, perch covers, claw clippers, and toys are available at pet shops that normally sell live birds.

level below freezing. Metal is a first-class conductor of both heat and cold.

The advantages of the box-type cage are obvious. If the dimensions which have already been referred to are borne in mind, this cage provides a home for your birds which one can guarantee to be draught-proof, and in it there is much more opportunity for a bird to find comparative seclusion if that is what it desires. A bird that is sitting on the perch as far away from the wire front as possible often seems to feel a sense of security which is never possible in an open cage.

It is usual to have cages of the box type painted on the inside in white and on the outside in black, but, although that may be the conventional color pattern, it is not necessarily the best and is definitely not the most attractive. In fact, there is a very strong argument for having the inside white and the outside of some light color rather than the conventional black. Cream on the outside, with white inside, makes everything look so much lighter even if this may be only self-deception.

Since lovebirds have an insatiable impulse to chew, it is extremely important that the paint used should be lead-free. This is readily available on the market. Any paint that is listed as non-toxic or safe for children is also safe for lovebirds. And it is wise to use such paint anywhere in the area where birds that slip out of the cage unobserved might be able to chew until caught and returned to the cage. Lead paint should never be used in the bird room.

CAGE BOTTOMS

It does not matter whether the cage is an all-wire one or one of the box type, there should always be a removable tray in it so that cleaning is made a much more simple task. A metal tray, usually of zinc, is, in fact, quite a normal fitting for all cages. It is a simple matter then to remove the tray, replace the paper, and slide it back in with a minimum of disturbance to the birds.

Some fanciers prefer this sliding tray also to be painted, and, if this done, there are several advantages, particularly that of preventing rust. Generally speaking, painted trays have a much longer life provided that any bare patches are repainted as often as necessary.

WIRE FRONTS

For lovebirds it is most important to consider the space between the separate wires of the cage front. A normal size is 1/2 in. spaces. For larger birds, of course, it can be as much as 5/8 in. Great care has to be taken to see that the fitting of the perches does not increase the space between the wires.

CAGE FITTINGS: FOOD AND WATER DISHES

There are quite a large number of fanciers who make their own cages and aviaries, but perhaps a considerable majority of those who keep birds buy their equipment because they are not handy with tools. When this is the case, the arrangement of the fittings is something which should be decided before a purchase is made. There are, however, a number of points to consider, and the beginner certainly must think about these when he goes to a dealer to choose any cage.

The two essential fittings are food and water cups. These should be of a type which is convenient for the person who is going to attend to the birds—that means that they must be placed where they are easily accessible and be made of a material which is easily cleaned. Right-angled corners are much less easy to clean than those that are rounded.

Probably the best way to arrange both feeding and water dishes is to hang them on the inside of a small door. These are what are known as turn-out feeders. You open the door and swivel it on its hinge and the food dish is immediately accessible. It can be lifted out of its slot or the holes into which it is fixed, then the door is shut again while the dish itself is taken away for cleaning and refilling.

It should be regarded as quite definite that the day of the feed or water container outside the cage, to reach which the bird has to push its head through a hole in the wire, is long since past. There is just nothing to recommend dishes of this sort at all, and no bird ought to be expected to push its head through any hole to reach either food or water.

PERCHES

The next essential for the cage is perches.

Cage birds spend by far the greater part of their time on perches unless they belong to those rather unusual species which are accustomed in their native state to pass most of their time on the ground. However, none of the birds dealt with in this book is of that kind, for the lovebirds described here are essentially perching birds.

It is quite natural, of course, that perches should be of certain standard patterns and sizes, but what also becomes quite obvious, when one thinks about it, is that birds are not themselves of standard size. Between the smallest and the largest lovebirds there is a very great difference in size, which of course means a very considerable variation in foot size. Thus, perches must always be chosen to suit the feet of the bird. It is just one of those things which one learns from experience by looking into the cage and watching the birds when they are on the perches. One can see whether they are grasping the perch with their claws and toes in a comfortable manner or not. If the perches are wrong, they should be changed without delay. The most commonly used size would be about one-half inch in diameter.

There is a point, however, that should be made here. It is that all cages should have several perches of different diameter. The largest, of course, should be of a size easily grasped by the bird without stretching its feet uncomfortably, but there should also be smaller perches. The reason is simply due to the fact that for a bird to keep its feet in the same position for hour after hour can become very tiring, while a variation in perch size does allow the feet to relax.

SEED HOPPERS

There are fanciers who prefer seed hoppers to dishes. Hoppers have the very definite advantage that, being covered on top, the birds are not able to foul the seed easily. Naturally, when arranging the perches, care must be taken to see that they are fixed in such a way that it is as difficult as possible for the droppings to get onto the seed when it is kept in open containers.

There is, however, one very distinct disadvantage with hoppers unless a good deal of observation is exercised. The idea of the hopper is not only that it keeps the seed clean, but that it saves labor in that several days' seed supply can be put in at one time. When this is done, there is a possibility that although the hopper may appear to be well supplied with seed, all that the birds can actually reach are the husks they have left behind, while they cannot, in fact, get at the seed at all. This danger can be removed by taking out the hoppers each day and blowing away the husks that have accumulated. If you neglect to do this, your birds may have days of frustration and hunger.

Hoppers for lovebirds present problems not involved with other species of cage birds. If constructed of wood the hoppers are subject to formidable attacks by sturdy beaks, and if the seed mixture contains large sunflower seeds, they are more readily subject to clogging at the opening of the hopper.

Quite serviceable hoppers can be bought in poultry or rabbit-supply stores. They are made of metal and have rather wide mouths for the flow of feed. It still is wise, however, to check the supply frequently to be sure that the birds have food available.

AVIARIES

Although the greater number of lovebirds kept are housed in cages, in many cases because their owners lack sufficient space to build an aviary, there are, nevertheless, many hundreds of fanciers who have a suitable garden in which a most attractive aviary can be built. Some of these may have no aviary because they cannot face the expense, but there are still many more who actually prefer to keep their birds in cages.

There is really very little that one can say about the indoor aviary except that it is a large cage capable of housing more birds than one is likely to be able to care for satisfactorily in the normal type of stock cage. Indoor aviaries, too, are usually larger than any normal type of cage, and have definitely the one advantage that they do permit the birds to take much more exercise because there is more flying space.

It is not intended in this chapter to give detailed instructions as to how aviaries should be built, whether they are of the indoor type or the more normal outdoor variety. It is most important to make up one's mind as to the exact type of aviary that one wants, but before coming to such a decision, there are certain points which have to be borne in mind. Perhaps the most important of these is the health of the lovebirds, for the pleasure or disappointment which the birdkeeper himself achieves depends upon the fitness and long life of his birds. He can have a most attractive aviary to look at, but it is useless if it does not provide an environment that is hygenic. In this connection the type of floor used is of great importance.

Even now, with all that has been written on the subject, and despite the fact that those with considerable experience in birdkeeping have pointed out the dangers, it is not at all uncommon to see a small aviary in a back garden with an earth floor. If one talks to the owner, there is usually a tale to be told of regular loss of birds from disease over a considerable period. Earth floors are extremely dangerous for the simple reason that they are difficult to clean and cannot fail to become polluted in time by the birds' droppings. One sick bird may, through contaminating an earth floor, pass on disease to other birds which may be put into the same aviary several months later.

There are many aviaries with wooden floors, and these are certainly better than bare earth, although they also have their disadvantages. They become wet, the boards warp, and it must be remembered also that wood can become a source of disease unless it is frequently scrubbed and disinfected. On the other hand, cement can be dealt with much more easily from the hygienic point of view. Such floors can be washed over frequently, and provided that suitable drainage has been arranged, no surplus water will lie on the surface for a sufficient time to cause discomfort or possible danger to the birds.

One great disadvantage with a concrete-floored aviary is that the expense of putting it down means that it has to be used for a long time or else the expenditure is not worthwhile. From the artistic point of view, too, concrete has little to recommend it, and it is impossible to grow any grass in it, so that, if there are to be any plants or shrubs, they will have to be grown in boxes. For the fixed aviary, however, a concrete floor is the one to be recommended every time.

The ideal aviary from the point of view of the birds is one which is movable, for after it has been used for one season on any particular piece of ground, it can be shifted on to a fresh piece for the next breeding season. If this is done, there is very little risk of disease through contaminated soil or grass. Naturally, movable aviaries must be constructed very solidly or they will soon begin to disintegrate if frequently moved. It is difficult to grow bushes in a movable aviary, but by no means impossible.

From the artistic point of view, a large planted aviary is the ideal, but if this type of aviary is used over a period of years and the number of birds kept in it is not restricted to a very small number, even there the ground will become foul, and the plants may not only be mutilated but also become covered with droppings. It is a fact, however, and one which has been learned by constant experience by those who have tried to breed some of the more difficult species, that there is little hope of success unless the breeding operations are planned in a well-planted aviary where conditions approach as nearly as possible the state of nature to which the birds were originally accustomed.

Here, then, a number of important considerations have been put before those who intend to have an aviary in their garden. Which type they will choose will depend to a certain extent upon circumstances of space, but probably also on the contents of their purse. In these days a well-constructed aviary of considerable size is expensive.

THE AVIARY

The normal aviary consists of two parts: a flight and a shelter. The flight must be considerably larger than the shelter because it is in this section that the birds will take their exercise. How the space is divided between flight and aviary

An aviary constructed as an addition to a garage in an urban setting.

will depend upon a number of factors. In the first place, from the bird's point of view, the longer the flight the better, and if the aviary is a comparatively small one, at least four-fifths of the total length should be given up to the flight. But here a difficulty is created for the owner because it leaves him with a shelter which is very small, and from his point of view attending to the birds will always be difficult unless he has sufficient elbow room. In small aviaries of this type it is usual to gain access to the shelter by standing in the flight itself, for there is rarely room to make an outside door convenient.

Thus, probably the first thing to do is to decide on the

length of flight that is necessary for the birds to keep them in sound condition, and then after that to consider the type and size of the shelter, each of which points will be governed by the available space and the cost. Many fanciers like their shelter in the form of a bird-room so that when the inmates have been driven in from the flight they, the owners, can sit down and watch their pets in the inside cages or small flights. If a shelter of this sort is within the means of the bird-keeper, it is certainly the one which will give him the greatest pleasure in his hobby.

SUITABLE SITES

An aviary should be placed in such a position that the lovebirds will get the maximum of winter sunshine. That does not imply that it must be placed in such a way that the sun can glare down on the birds at midday on the hottest summer day without their being able to find any protection for themselves. Birds love sunshine, but many people who are not fanciers at all will have noticed that in the full heat of a summer day birds seem to disappear. They like to get into the shade for a time, and many of them rest for perhaps an hour or more in the middle part of the day.

Nevertheless sunshine must be available, even if protection against it when it is extreme also has to be considered. In the Northern Hemisphere, the aviary should face in a southerly direction. Probably it is better that it should not receive, over the whole length of the flight, full sunshine at midday, so it is often a good plan to face it towards the south-west.

THE FLIGHT

In exposed places it is unwise to have the flight covered with wire netting on all three sides. If it is known that prevailing winds which are cold come from a particular quarter, that side of the flight should be boarded up. In fact, there is probably much to be said for at least one side, if not two, being completely covered. It is a mistake, however, to cover the top completely, for it is of great value to birds not only to have direct sunshine but also to be able occasionally to let rain fall on their feathers. Very few birds like to re-

main out in a downpour, so to save them from having to retire into the shelter a small portion of the flight near the
shelter can be roofed over.

To be strictly honest in this matter, however, it ought to
be stated that there are breeders of considerable experience
who will not under any circumstances have any part of the
flight covered at all. The beginner will naturally learn from
experience which method of protection he finds more satisfactory in practice, but it will do no harm to start off with
part of the flight covered.

VERMIN

One of the bugbears that the bird-keeper has to endure
is the presence of rats and mice. Wherever there are seed-
eating birds, in a comparatively short space of time both
these pests will put in an appearance. Rats are particularly
unpleasant and can cause serious harm to birds of almost any
size. In fact, it is very likely that if rats get into either the
shelter or the flight, some of the inmates will be killed. They
must therefore be kept out at all costs. Although that advice
may sound comparatively easy to achieve, it is by no means
so unless one takes very careful precautions. Naturally rats
cannot get through 4 in. of concrete, and so an aviary which
has this depth of concrete under the flight and also under the
shelter is more or less immune from them. But, even so, the
bird-keeper has to keep his eye on the woodwork of shelter
and flight to see that this is not attacked, because even if one
of these rodents does not get in the first night, if it has started
to make a hole it will certainly gain entrance during the second night and the consequences may be disastrous.

If the floor is not made of concrete, then other precautions are necessary, and the only thing to do is to fringe both
shelter and flight with wire netting to a depth of at least 2 ft.
This means digging a trench of sufficient depth, but also
wide enough to allow the wire netting to be bent outwards.
The rats then, burrowing down, will come in contact with
the wire and in all probability will not be able to get through
before the hole in the ground has been noticed and refilled
with materials which rats find unpleasant.

Mice, although they are not as dangerous, can be a very great nuisance, and are even more difficult to keep out of the aviary. Mice can, with ease, squeeze their way through wire netting of 1/2 in. mesh, and small mice can get through even the smallest mesh which is generally available, in fact, as small as 3/8 in. However, every attempt must be made to keep mice out, particularly when breeding operations are in progress, for although they are not likely to injure adult birds, they will, without doubt, frighten them, and if they get into a nest, may kill or turn out the babies which are not yet fledged. Adult birds which are scared at night often do themselves serious injury by dashing into the wooden walls. And rat or mouse droppings are poisonous to birds, so if a rodent does not actually disturb the birds in the flight he may foul their food.

The bird-keeper is always at his wit's end in trying to prevent mice from getting into either the shelter or the flight, and it is only by persistence that finally he becomes reasonably successful. Mice find it extremely difficult to run up glass, and sheet metal presents a similar difficult foothold. Thus, if the bottom of the flight is surrounded by sheets of metal to a height of 12 to 15 in., there is every chance of success in keeping these little pests outside. One also has to bear in mind the fact that if mice do get in from time to time they must be prevented from reaching the food dishes. To achieve this object all dishes, whether containing food or water, should be placed on stands with flat and projecting tops. Such stands can be supported by a central post, and if the board on which the pots rest is about 2 ft. square, no mice will get onto the top unless they drop down onto it from the roof. Surprisingly as it may seem, mice can do this, and they can then jump several feet to the ground without injuring themselves in the least.

VENTILATION

Naturally the flight provides no ventilation problem, but the shelter requires well-thought-out ventilation with an inlet low down and protected against mice, and an outlet on the opposite wall near the eaves. By careful thought this inlet and outlet can be so arranged that there is no possibility of the birds' being in a draught, but it is most important that on hot summer days there should be a free current of air through the shelter. This is perhaps even more important at night when all the birds will be in the shelter. It is also an advantage, too, to have windows that open. The window spaces must be protected by wire netting so that the birds cannot escape.

At all times glass must be covered with 1/2 in. wire netting because birds cannot see glass and will fly into it head-first and do themselves considerable damage unless it is made visible to them.

POPHOLES

The space through which the birds enter the shelter from the flight is sometimes called the *pophole*. Occasionally the word *'bobhole'* is used.

It is essential that the birds should spend the night in the shelter, and when they are unaccustomed to their surroundings, the task of getting them in is not always easy. For this reason a good deal of thought has to be paid both to the situation and to the size of the pophole. It is not unusual, during the first few days after a number of fresh birds have been introduced, to have to drive them into the shelter at night, and this can be a very difficult job. Behaving from what can only be instinct, they always try to get as high up as possible. Normally popholes are not put right at the top of the division between the flight and the shelter, but it is an excellent idea to have a hole here, either as a temporary measure in addition to the ordinary bobhole, or if one wishes it, as a permanent part of the arrangement of the aviary. Certainly it is far less trouble to get birds in when the entrance is right at the very top.

If birds which have been living in an aviary for some time are disinclined to go into the shelter, that is almost certainly due to the fact that the shelter is not light enough. Birds object very strongly to going into the dark, and so it is of great importance that a shelter should be light enough to attract them. So light, in fact, that they do not notice any

Low single doors allow entrance to these partitioned outdoor aviaries.

real difference between the conditions in the flight and those in the shelter into which they are expected to retire at dusk.

There are various devices which can be used to shut the pophole through which the birds go in and out from the shelter to the flight. The simplest, from the point of view of the operator, is one which can be manipulated without having to go into the aviary at all. It will not tax the ingenuity of the handyman, and certainly not of the aviary manufacturer, to produce a slide which can be pushed to close the entrance when all the birds have gone in safely for the night.

DOORS

In most cases there is a door attached to the flight and another to the shelter. In the case of the shelter there is no real difficulty at all because the birds are either caged or in a flight space well protected by wire netting. With the door in the aviary, however, it is another matter, and it is essential that precautions should be taken to see that as one enters the birds, which may be temporarily frightened, do not escape. This can be achieved comparatively simply by having a low-down door, not more than 3 ft. high. When there is a door of this sort, it takes into account the normal behavior of love-birds, which are accustomed to fly upwards rather than downwards when they are approached. It may be a little inconvenient for the owner to have to stoop so low to get in. The only advantage of a door of this sort is that it does save a little on the initial cost of building an aviary. Generally speaking, however, it is much better to have a safety porch, which is, in fact, a small addition to the flight, with its own entrance. The owner opens a wire netting door, goes into a small enclosure, and then shuts this outside door behind him. After that is done, he is quite safe in opening the interior door which leads directly into the flight. When there is a safety porch, there is very little danger of birds escaping when their aviary is being attended to, unless the owner is unusually careless.

An outdoor aviary having doors of normal dimensions. Notice the small triangular area that is created in one corner of the flight, at the point of entrance. Photo by R.C. Mowle.

2: Buying Birds

The only sensible approach to the hobby of bird-keeping is to have the accommodation ready before there is any serious thought of purchasing any birds. It is more than probable that the species to be kept will have been decided while the accommodation is being prepared, but it would be unwise to consider taking delivery of the birds until full preparations have been made to house them.

It sometimes happens that a would-be fancier is presented with birds. Then his situation is somewhat complicated, for he just has to make do. It may be necessary for him to improvise a temporary cage, but this is definitely not the ideal approach to the hobby.

There are various ways in which lovebirds can be purchased, and there is something to be said for each of them. But here a word of warning must be given to the beginner. If he knows nothing about foreign birds at all, his first step should be to join a local bird club if he can, and to make contact with some local fancier whom he can visit, and who will give him much more practical advice in a few minutes than he will be able to learn from any book in a matter of hours.

The most complete source of information regarding other fanciers is *American Cage-Bird Magazine*, 3449 North Western Avenue, Chicago, Ill. 60618. It is the most widely circulated publication available. It lists the places and times of the monthly meetings of most of the local bird clubs in North America, which is the richest pool of information for new fanciers. In addition it lists the specialist societies and carries relevant articles and advertisements of all sorts related to cage birds.

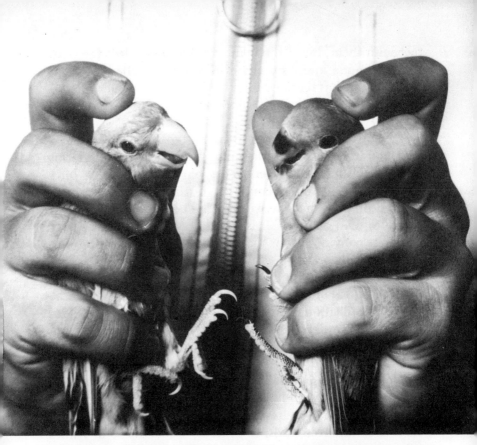

A fully mature Peach-faced Lovebird (left) contrasted with a juvenile bird. Notice that the younger bird still maintains a good amount of dark coloring on its bill; as the bird ages, the bill gradually becomes lighter, and the feathering on the head becomes progressively rosier in color. Photo by Miceli Studios.

Many people who buy birds study the advertisement columns. A beginner will have no knowledge at all of the people who are advertising stock for sale, but it is just at this point that the established fancier's experience can be of real assistance. He will undoubtedly have purchased birds in the past from some of the people who are advertising stock and will be able to recommend those who have given him complete satisfaction. With regard to others, he may have nothing to say at all, probably because he has never made contact with them, but if the man who has kept birds for years and has made many purchases has been satisfied with the treatment he has received from any particular dealer, the beginner who receives such information should certainly act upon it.

Naturally some species travel better than others, and it is a good idea to know something about this before ordering birds which have to travel over a long distance. Such birds might arrive in sound condition during the summer, but could be in poor shape in winter. The best dealers, of course, refuse to send delicate birds over long distances unless they are quite convinced that they are more or less certain to arrive in sound condition.

One important point always to bear in mind when making a purchase of lovebirds is that the lowest price is not always an indication of the birds that are cheapest in the long run. If the same species is offered at widely different prices, there is very probably a reason for this difference. Obviously birds which have very recently been acquired ought to be cheaper than those which have been in the dealer's hands for some time and which he has partially, if not completely, acclimatized. Birds that have been bred in this country are preferable to imported birds. In general, it is better to buy stock from the person who raised it or from his retail agent.

Sometimes birds are purchased and things start to go wrong immediately. If the buyer is a fancier of little experience, he is inclined to reach the conclusion that he has been cheated and that all bird-dealers are rogues. Nothing could be further from the truth.

Those publications which accept advertisements are very careful to exclude from their columns any dealers who have proved to be consistently unsatisfactory, and it is fundamentally true that the dealers who treat beginners with scant consideration are so small in number that they can safely be ignored.

Undoubtedly the best way of buying birds is to see them and choose them at local petshops that may occasionally have lovebirds. Petshop operators may also be willing to order them from the breeders or other dealers for you. If an experienced fancier can be persuaded to make the visit and help in the choice, so much the better, but it often happens that birds have to be chosen entirely as a result of one's own decision. It is then a wise plan, when going to buy birds, to tell the dealer as soon as you arrive that you want to look around, and explain to him that if he is busy he can get on with his own work while you look carefully at the birds which interest you.

CHOOSING A HEALTHY BIRD

There are very definite signs of fitness for which a purchaser should look. Unless he sees these signs in the birds in front of him, he should come away without them. It is quite useless to buy birds about which one feels doubtful, and it is unsatisfactory to the dealer who may later receive a complaint. To say the least, careless selection is unwise from the point of view of the buyer who gets home with his birds and then, within a few days, finds that his new purchases die.

The experienced fancier is not unduly impressed by the feather condition of the lovebirds at which he is looking. His trained eye may tell why the birds look rough, and why perhaps they are short of feathers in places where he would hope to find them in full feather. The beginner, however, has not this experience, and it is wise for him to make his choice from birds which are in excellent plumage, tight of feather and bright of color if brightness of color is a characteristic of the species.

The first thing to do is to stand away from the birds and to watch them from a distance. Normally, if one walks straight up to a cage, it becomes impossible to see anything except that the birds are alarmed and quite unnatural. Birds in that state give no clear indication of either health or sickness.

It is a good plan, too, to keep an eye on the food pots. Those birds which go down to the pots and eat away with appetite are unlikely to be badly out of condition, but you sometimes see other birds which, although they are constantly by the seed and peck at it in a desultory fasion, do not act-

The feet of a psittacine bird with arthritis. This condition can indicate the presence of other diseases as well as simple old age. Photo from the T.F.H. Publications book *Bird Diseases*, by Arnall and Keymer.

ually eat anything at all. These birds are the ones to be avoided.

In practically every large batch of birds that you are likely to see, one or two of them will be on the perches with their heads under their wings and both feet firmly planted on the perch. That is definitely not an indication of fitness. They probably need to stand on two feet because they are weak. Birds, when they first arrive at a petshop, are exhausted, and probably hungry as well, and may for a short time act in this way. If they are essentially fit, they should recover in a day or two.

When you have watched the birds in which you are interested for a few minutes and have decided on several which you think are hopeful, that is the time to ask the dealer if he will get them for you. You should then inspect them at close quarters.

First of all the eyes should be inspected very carefully. The bird with a bright and clean eye probably has very little wrong with it, but if the eyes are watery or there is any discharge of any kind, or, as often happens, one eye is closed, then such lovebirds should be rejected.

However, before you actually agree to buy them, you should look at the vent. If the vent is gummed up, which in itself may not indicate any serious disease, there is still no need to take any chances. A clean vent is always preferable to one that is dirty. The experienced fancier, by looking at the vent, can often tell whether the trouble is the result of digestive disorder or merely that the bird has got soiled through the fact that it has probably been kept under crowded conditions in an unsuitable travelling box. The beginner does not possess this skill.

The next thing to do is to look at the feet, because so often birds are found to have defective feet. It may sound rather stupid, but it is important that you should actually make sure that all the toes are present. If the dealer has noticed that a toe is missing, he will only offer that bird for sale at a much reduced price, for a sound pair of feet is an essential!

If you have been as thorough as this in the selection of you lovebirds, you may have caused the dealer some trouble, but he will not mind that if he feels that you have been intelligent and are trying to make a reasonable start, thus preventing trouble for yourself and providing him with a future customer.

3: Acclimatization

The word 'acclimatization' really means much more than getting foreign birds used to your local climate. Adjustment to unusual temperatures is, of course, important for some species which come from tropical lands and are delicate. Generally speaking the word implies a method of treatment which allows these birds to become accustomed to an environment which is entirely different from that which they have experienced in their native haunts. Few species can be provided with exactly the same food which it has been their habit to find for themselves in their own country, and it thus becomes the task of the person who is acclimatizing them to get them on to those foods for captive birds which are easily available.

When first placed in cages, lovebirds are naturally easily alarmed, and it is only by the patience of the person who is looking after them that they will, in a comparatively short time, settle down and become steady. For this purpose it is a sound idea to put lovebirds in comparatively small cages at first. The dealer cannot afford either the space or the cages for such care, but the purchaser who is the bird-fancier will find that many species which are extremely wild when he first gets them become reasonably tame if they are treated with care and consideration; also if a determined and patient attempt is made to win their confidence. The period of time spent in a cage is valuable, too, in that it allows the owner to inspect the birds very carefully for possible signs of ill-health.

Another aspect of acclimatization is that it provides isolation from birds which have been in the fancier's possession for some time and are known to be fit. There are a number of bird diseases which do not immediately show themselves, and two to three weeks in a cage (as a minimum) will ensure

Agapornis roseicollis, the Peach-faced Lovebird. Photo by Harry V. Lacey.

that the new birds, when they are finally added to a collection, will be unlikely to be carriers of disease.

Generally speaking, temperature is not of great importance as far as lovebirds are concerned, provided that they are not subjected to extreme cold. They come from tropical countries where the day temperature reaches a very high level, but they have, during their short lives, grown accustomed to the rapid and considerable falls in temperature which occur at night. Ordinary living-room temperatures are quite satisfactory for most lovebird species. (It is an entirely different matter when one decides to keep some of the softbills which must be kept in temperatures on the order of 80° F when first imported, but the care of softbills is not within the scope of this book.)

Were it possible, it would always be wise to buy lovebirds in the spring, so that after a few weeks in which to settle them down, and to allow them to become accustomed to unusual foods, they could be put outside in the aviary or mixed with established birds in the cages of the birdroom. Unfortunately, that is not always possible.

Perhaps the proof of satisfactory treatment of new birds is how they fare during their first molt. That is very often a critical time, but if it is surmounted without undue difficulty, then from that time onwards there should be no further trouble, provided that sound common-sense methods are the normal practice of the fancier. No matter what the species, carelessness and a failure to attend to detail always bring in their train inevitable disappointment and disaster.

New birds which arrive exhausted should always be put in a temperature higher than that which will later be normal for them. For several days they may have been short of food, and they will have no body heat to spare.

As wide a variety as possible of suitable foods should be put before them, and this food must be placed where the birds are bound to see it. Several pots are certainly better than one at this time, and the same remark also applies to water dishes.

For the first day or two the cages in which new birds are housed should be approached only when necessary, but

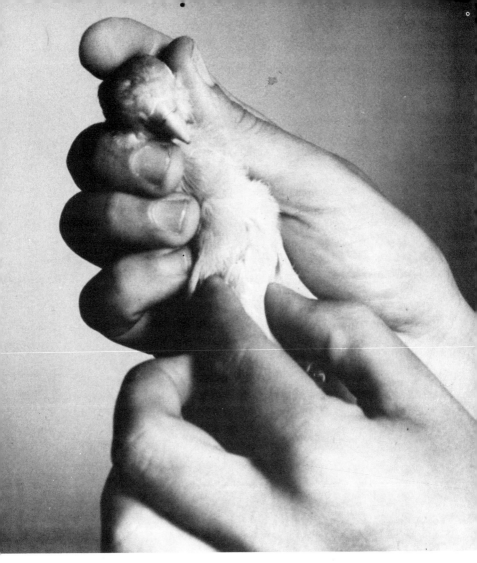

Examining a Peach-faced Lovebird to determine the relative "chest-iness" of the bird. The chest area should be plump and gently roun-ded; an examination that reveals a sharp keeled breastbone and comparatively steep angulation of the area around the bone is a sign that the bird needs good care to be returned to the best of health. Photo by Miceli Studios.

when they are eating well the same care not to alarm them will be unnecessary, for by this time the business of acclimat-ization will be well under way.

Fischer's Lovebird (upper bird) and Peach-faced Lovebird, as rendered by R.A. Vowles.

Opposite:
Fischer's Lovebird, *Agapornis fischeri*. Photo by Harry V. Lacey.

4: Water

It is impossible to over-emphasize the importance of water in bird-keeping because all birds, unless they are almost entirely fruit-eating, insectivorous or nectar-feeding, drink quite a considerable quantity of water in the course of a day. Naturally, during those times of the year when there is a wide variety of popular green food available, the amount of water needed will be less. However, perhaps even more important than clean seed is fresh drinking water which should be kept in dishes which cannot possibly become fouled. Water into which the droppings of birds fall becomes a very probable source of disease.

The position of the water cups is also important for another reason, because the birds soon show that water which has been allowed to stand for some hours in full sunshine is much less palatable than that which has been kept in the shade. At all times water containers should be filled at least once a day, and, during hot weather, it is a good idea to give water as many times as is convenient. When the water dish is emptied, it should always be cleaned before it is refilled.

Water is also valuable for another reason based on the fact that it is the natural instinct of birds to bathe. The majority of birds which are kept in captivity enjoy bathing, and some of them are prepared to soak themselves many times during the day. It may perhaps seem strange, but birds as an animal group appear to be extremely particular about the cleanliness of the water which they use for bathing, and they object to bathing in dirty water and will only do so if no other is available.

In an aviary it is usually extremely simple to put a large dish on a stand, and it is interesting from the point of view of the owner to stand by and watch his birds bathing themsel-

A budgie being given its bath. The same spraying technique can be used to bathe a lovebird that does not bathe itself. Photo by Louise Van der Meid.

ves, and then afterwards preening their feathers with great vigor and thoroughness. No bird ever looks in really fine feather unless it gets an opportunity to wash itself and then to carry out this specialized toilet with its beak.

Although most lovebird species are enthusiastic bathers, there are individual birds which object very strongly to getting into the water which is provided for them, probably because they have some suspicion of the container. When that is the case, they may have to be sprayed. During the winter time they may still have to be sprayed, but with water that is really hot. By the time this water has been atomized to a very fine spray it is not at all hot, and will certainly do no harm. Cold water, on the other hand, may produce a chill.

Top to bottom: Red-rumped Parrot, *Psephotus haematonotus;* lutino variety of the Nyasaland Lovebird, *Agapornis lilianae;* Blue-masked Lovebird. Drawing by R.A. Vowles.

Black-masked Lovebird. Photo by Mueller-Schmida.

5: Feeding

The importance of correct feeding for lovebirds cannot be over-emphasized, for to mention one point alone, their resistance is quickly lowered if the diet they receive is unsatisfactory. Lowered resistance produced by malnutrition means that they are more likely to develop diseases of various kinds, and all who have kept birds must have realized how quickly they can die when they are out of condition. It is, however, a cheering fact that sound condition can be promoted by right methods of feeding. The experienced fancier has learned this fact very early on in his career, but there is no reason at all why the beginner should not have at his disposal sufficient information to make it possible for him to feed his birds on the right lines from the start.

The satisfactory nutrition of lovebirds is a complicated business scientifically, but quite simply it means that different types of feeding matter must be present in the diet that is provided. Certain elements are essential for correct feeding. The word 'element' is not used in its scientific sense but is an expression to cover the different types of food which may be found in a particular item of diet, the carbohydrates, the proteins, the fats, the vitamins, the minerals, all of which in one way or another are essential to good health. Very few foods contain all these groups, but a variety of food can cover the whole list. Now it is not necessary for the bird-fancier to sit down to calculate calories, which is often the lot of those who have to feed human beings, because in the case of lovebirds correct feeding can usually be achieved by providing a wide variety of different foods. The wider this variety the greater the chance there is that all the essentials of a correct feeding will have been covered.

When talking of the feeding of lovebirds, one rarely

considers how much food should be given, for the simple reason that there is always a tendency to put before them more than an adequate supply. Thus, the only caution that has to be given from time to time is that certain items of food should be limited in quantity, usually because of their fattening effect, an effect which will not be as noticeable with birds which have ample exercise as in the case of those which are confined in a comparatively small space. The feeding of fattening foods which can affect the liver may have fatal results unless their quantity is strictly limited.

SEEDS

All lovebirds are seed-eaters. That does not mean that they eat nothing but seed, but their main item of diet is seed and usually consists of several different types. Birds have their likes and dislikes and usually show a preference for one type of seed over some of the others. Thus it is a sound idea to provide the seeds which are suited to the inmates of either cage or aviary in separate pots so that the birds can take what they want without having to search through the mixture to find what they like, and throw out, as they will do, what they have no use for at the moment. There are many fanciers who do not believe in separate containers for seeds, and if anyone feels that way he can put his mixture in the dishes. Perhaps he has no need to worry unduly about the seed which gets thrown on to the floor of the cage or aviary, for the chances are that where a number of birds are kept together what one bird wastes another bird may immediately pick up.

QUALITY OF SEED

The quality of the seed provided for birds is of great importance, and it is always wiser to go to dealers who are known to be very careful preparers of seed. If only one or two birds are kept, it is probably that the seed mixture will be bought in packet form, and packet seeds are usually prepared by firms who have great experience, and perhaps what is even more important, a long-standing reputation to main-

Blue-masked Lovebirds perched on a conifer stump. Photo by Mueller-Schmida.

Opposite:
Agapornis fischeri,
Fischer's Lovebird. This
colorful and attractive
species is second in
availability to the Peach-
faced Lovebird and its color
varieties. Photo by
Harry V. Lacey.

tain. Dirty seed is always dangerous, and so care should be taken to see that any seed mixture has been carefully cleaned, and anything which could have contaminated it has been removed. Don't buy birdseed at a supermarket. It's too rarely fresh. Buy seed at petshops.

VARIETIES OF SEEDS

One of the most popular seeds is yellow millet, which comes from India, although there are other parts of the world, such as Australia, where it is grown. It is this seed which is extremely popular with even the smallest birds, and they will eat it usually in preference to anything else.

White millet is also valuable, and is a great favorite with birds which are able to husk it easily. It is a valuable food because there is much more kernel than husk.

Canary seed is also another great favorite with those birds which have either known it in the wild or have quickly learned to appreciate it in captivity. Canary comes from various parts of the world, and quality and size vary considerably. It has a very high feeding value.

Millet in spray form may be rather expensive, but it is well worth feeding. If they have the choice of millet in a dish or millet in the spray in which it was grown, they will certainly choose the spray first.

From experience bird-fanciers have found that spray millet is a great conditioner. Why this should be so is not absolutely certain, but it has been suggested on a number of occasions that there is something in the husk of spray millet which is extremely valuable from a nutritional point of view. Some of the husk is certainly eaten, and it may be that either vitamins or minerals which are absent from ordinary seed mixtures can be found in this husk, which is, therefore, of benefit to the birds.

It is usual to feed the seeds which have already been mentioned in a dry state, but there is something to be said for providing sprouted seed also. Many birds in the wild like to scratch about on the ground and to pick up seed which has dropped from grasses and has started to germinate in the ground. Seed in this state is certainly richer in vitamins than

There are many different seeds and seed mixtures available as staple foods for lovebirds, and there are many items that can be fed as occasional treats. Large-scale keepers of birds usually buy seeds in bulk, but owners of a single bird or just a few birds find it more economical to purchase packaged seeds and treats in small quantities, thereby assuring freshness and avoiding storage problems.

Agapornis taranta, the Abyssinian Lovebird, also called Black-winged Lovebird. Photo by Mueller-Schmida.

Opposite:
A pair of Abyssinian
Lovebirds. The male has a
red band across the crown.
Drawing by R.A. Vowles.

dried seed, but it does lose some of its protein value when it has sprouted.

Particularly during the wintertime, when green food may be short, there is a very strong argument for feeding sprouted seed from time to time. The actual business of sprouting seed is not at all difficult. A cup of seed placed in warm water and left for 24 hours is referred to as "soaked seed" and is an excellent tonic. When left in the water or laid on moist blotter or cloth until it sprouts it makes an even more nourishing food. Some prefer to sprout it in moist soil.

There are fanciers who throw down seed on the floor of their aviary, where in time some of it germinates and is picked up by the birds. There are birds, in fact, which prefer to pick up their food from the ground, but on the whole, unless one can be quite sure that the seed thrown down is not likely to be polluted by the bird's droppings, this method of feeding has little to recommend it.

Hemp is another seed which is used for the larger birds, but should only be given in small quantities. It is available in North America only in sterile form, since it is the seed of marihuana. Only pet shops with large volume are likely to have it. It is especially rich in oil and in the winter is an excellent addition to the diet.

It is a good idea to give some sunflower to lovebirds each day, and then from time to time to allow them to eat as much as they want just for one day. After that feast they should again be rationed. There is a tendency for all seeds to deteriorate the longer they are kept, and there is definitely sound sense in getting a supply of the new season's crop every year.

GREEN FOOD

The most popular form of green food is seeding grasses, and for certain periods of the year it is a comparatively simple matter to provide a number of different varieties of such grasses and to tie them to bunches to be suspended in either the aviary or the cage where the birds can get at them easily.

Unfortunately, seeding grasses are not available all the year round, and the fancier is compelled to rely on substitute green foods, some of which are, however, quite popular. Spinach and spinach beet are frequently eaten with eagerness, and lettuce, although it is doubtful whether it has a great deal of feeding value, is rarely neglected by birds that like green food with fleshy leaves. Those garden greens which have been sprayed with various chemicals should be regarded with suspicion.

Whole books have been written on the subject of wild green foods which can be used in the feeding of birds, and those who are interested should obtain such books to see what a wide variety the countryside can provide for their birds. Chickweed, groundsel, dandelion and plantain are usually obtainable by anybody who does not live in the heart of a town. Some care must be taken to see that the wild green foods which are obtained have not been soiled by cats or dogs. Even more risky is the use of greens that might have been sprayed with insecticide. All greens that originate other than in a grocery store should be washed thoroughly before being used. This is because greens found at the shoulder of roads, etc., often have been sprayed with insecticides in an effort to prevent their wild growth.

Many birds are thrilled when a turf is put into their cage or aviary, particularly if the aviary happens to be one with a concrete floor. They not only like to eat the grass, but if it is wet, many birds will bathe themselves in it after they have finished eating all they need for the moment. A fresh turf several times a week is easily obtained and gives the birds pleasure as well as providing some small part of their diet.

Seed-eating birds on the whole are not fruit-eaters, but quite a number of species will eat apple, and some of them will even eat the more fleshy fruits. One never knows what one's birds will eat of foods of this sort until one has experimented with them, and the experiment is well worth trying.

ADDITIONS TO DIET

A valuable addition to diet for birds which are not kept in direct daylight and who get no actual sunshine at all is cod-liver oil. This is particularly valuable for birds which are kept in a cage in a living-room all the year round, and for

Peach-faced Lovebirds. Photo by Mueller-Schmida.

Deprived of their natural conditions, lovebirds and other captive bird species can benefit from the addition to their diet of vitamin and mineral supplements that help keep them in top condition. Many reliable products specifically designed for birds are available at pet supply stores.

those birds in an outside aviary whose flying in the open air has to be strictly limited during the winter months. The best way to feed cod-liver oil is to impregnate seed with it. This is quite a simple process. A pound jar of seed has carefully poured over the top of it a full teaspoonful of cod-liver oil. The jar is allowed to stand while the oil gradually percolates through the seed to the bottom. The best thing to do then is to remove the seed at the top, which will not be found to be too sticky, and to put it straight into the feeding pots. Seed which has been treated in this way can be fed throughout the winter if not more than one teaspoonful is used for each pound of seed. Naturally much of the oil will be wasted because the birds described in this book hardly eat any of the husk by intention, but they will get some of the cod-liver oil which will not only have got on to the husk, but will have found its way through into the kernel as well.

It is just possible that the providing of vitamin D in this way may make it necessary to increase the amount of vitamin E that the birds have in their diet. This need not be a serious problem, for there are a number of suitable vitamin mixtures on the market which can be fed to the birds to make sure that all their vitamin needs are supplied.

There is such a thing as vitamin poisoning, and it is a mistake to think that such compounds should be given every day. Twice a week is adequate, and will produce no ill effects, but may be very beneficial to the birds.

One other food ought to be mentioned here as an addition to diet, and that is the egg food which is so well known to the canary breeder. This food is very much appreciated by quite a number of lovebirds which are seed-eaters, and they will often eat it in considerable quantity when they have young in the nest. There are probably about as many formulas for egg food as there are canary fanciers, and most of them are well worth feeding. One very simple one is this: put hard-boiled eggs through a potato ricer, then add about one-fifth the volume with corn flake crumbs (from supermarket). Toss the mixture with a fork. Keep refrigerated until used.

Black-cheeked Lovebirds, *Agapornis nigrigensis.* Photo by Mueller-Schmida.

Opposite:
Nyasaland Lovebird (upper bird) and Black-cheeked Lovebird. Both of these species are comparatively rare, even though the Nyasaland Lovebird is a relatively free-breeding species in captivity. Drawing by R.A. Vowles.

Processed cuttlebones of the type sold for use with lovebirds and other species are easily attached to the bars of the cage and can be picked at whenever the birds feel like it. Photo by Miceli Studios.

Grit for lovebirds is available in a number of different mineral forms and grain sizes; be guided by the recommendation of the seller of the bird when selecting the type and size of grit to use. Photo by Miceli Studios.

DIGESTION

The digestion of a bird is a very complicated business, but that subject cannot be dealt with fully here. What must be said is that a bird has no teeth, and therefore it requires assistance in the grinding up of its food. This can be provided by sand and grit and powdered oyster shell. Probably the best way to supply the grinding tools for seed-eaters is to buy mineralized grit. This will carry out the mechanical job of crushing the seed in the gizzard and will also, because some of it is absorbed, provide the birds with some of the essential minerals which they require. Mineralized grits are cheap, and are probably better than anything one is likely to be able to provide by making up one's mixtures at home.

Just one word of warning is needed on the subject of grit. It is that those birds which have not been using it for some time should be limited rigorously in quantity. Grit when eaten to excess finds its way into the intestines and sets up serious irritation.

Cuttlebone, either in powdered form or as the actual skeleton of the squid, should always be available. Birds like cuttlebone, and apparently the calcium it contains is readily absorbed by them. Cuttlebone not only contains calcium, but it also contains salt, which is valuable in moderate quantity.

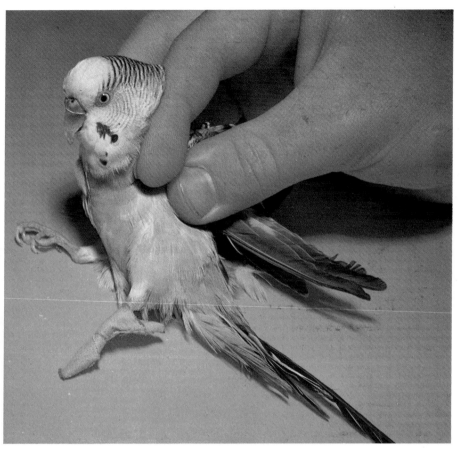

A budgerigar with a splinted leg covered with plaster of Paris and tape. Leg fractures are common among psittacine birds kept in cages having wire floors of the improper mesh size. Photo from *Bird Diseases,* by L. Arnall and I.F. Keymer.

Opposite:
Upper photo: A color mutation of the Peach-faced Lovebird. Called Golden Cherry Lovebird, this variety was developed in Japan. Photo by Louise Van der Meid.

Lower photo: Lovebirds in general are less easy to sex than many other psittacine birds. The Grand Eclectus Parrots shown here, for example, are easy to differentiate as to sex once they become adults. . . the male has green plumage, whereas the female is red and purple. Photo by Louise Van der Meid.

6:Diseases and Accidents

However careful the bird-owner may be, sooner or later he will experience disease among his stock, or it may be that some birds will become the victims of accident. For such contingencies as these he must be prepared. It would be quite wrong, however, to create the impression that disease is one of those misfortunes which is bound to strike seriously at some time or another and that there is nothing that can be done to prevent it. The extent of the seriousness of disease among birds kept in captivity always depends to a very large degree on the care which is bestowed upon the birds. The most important thing is *prevention*, and in many ways it is easier to prevent disease than it is to cure it. Birds are always difficult patients, and the amount of research which has been carried out with regard to the illnesses of birds is so small that the remedies one is compelled to employ become very largely empiric. What one man finds useful for his birds under certain conditions another finds quite useless.

Perhaps the greatest asset any bird-keeper can have is the ability to notice that a bird is unwell before it is, in fact, seriously ill. This 'stock sense' which some people possess to a very high degree is of the utmost value. On the other hand, there are some bird-keepers who do not realize that their birds are ill until they are almost at the point of death. When that stage is reached, the hopes of recovery must be extremely small.

Every day individual birds should be looked at, and any changes in appearance must be recognized. One of the best ways to prevent disease, of course, is strict cleanliness in cages, bird-room and aviary. The more the birds are allowed to clean themselves, and the more frequently the cages are cleaned, the less likelihood there is of trouble, particularly when it is an isolated bird which suddenly develops a disease which is later found to be infectious.

Newly imported birds are always a danger because one never knows what infection they may have been in contact with in the wild, and so, to prevent trouble, birds which are purchased, even from breeders in this country, should always be isolated for a time, perhaps for as long as two or three weeks, before they are put in with birds which are known to be fit. This statement has already been made in an earlier section of the book, but is so important that repetition here is not a mere waste of space.

SIGNS OF DISEASE

As has already been suggested, the bird-keeper should look to see if his birds appear fit. The bird which sits with its eyes closed is obviously unwell and should immediately be separated from the others. Any bird which is off its food is usually a sick bird, for as a rule the seed-eaters are almost continuous feeders. A bird which sits with its feathers all fluffed up is feeling the cold, probably because it has not been feeding and has thus been unable to maintain its body heat. It can reasonably be inferred from human experience that illness and feeling cold often go together.

The breathing of birds is hardly ever noticed when they are fit, but any bird that is sick may breathe with an irregular rhythm. It may also breathe noisily as well. Birds in this condition may be suffering from a variety of diseases, but it is essential that they should be isolated so that some treatment can be attempted. Warmth in such cases is always the first essential.

The presence of diarrhoea may be obvious from the droppings on the bottom of the cage, but when a number of birds are kept together, one has to look very carefully before finding the particular bird which is showing this symptom of ill-health. A bird that squats suddenly, twitches the tail, and appears to be attempting to pass something may be troubled with constipation. A collection of fecal matter around the vent is usually an indication that the bird is experiencing difficulties.

This lovebird has succumbed from alopecia, a fungal infection of the skin. Photo from *Bird Diseases*, by L. Arnall and I.F. Keymer.

Antibiotics specifically formulated for the treatment of bird ailments are valuable aids to bird keepers; before you medicate a bird, however, make sure you know the cause of the disease and its proper treatment—don't go in for the shotgun approach and medicate just on the basis that some medicine is better than none.

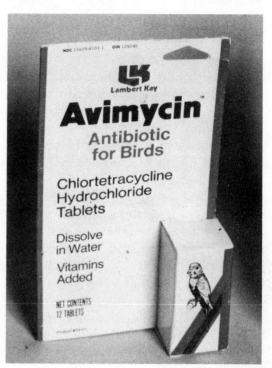

ANTIBIOTICS

Great advances have taken place in medicine in recent years with the development of antibiotics. Unfortunately, methods and dosages for cage birds have not yet received the attention of research scientists. We have the feeling that there is help for ill birds, but we do not have confidence in our ability to treat.

A few pharmaceutical houses have placed antibiotics on the market. These products are available at the pet shop. Dosage is important and directions should be followed carefully. Most of the remedies are administered in water, which means that all other water sources must be removed in order that the ill bird be forced to drink the medication. Forcing the medication into the beak is a last resort; the distress and energy loss caused by catching and holding the bird may do more harm than the weakened bird can take. Along with the medication heat should be applied.

THE VALUE OF HEAT

Perhaps the best remedy for all the ills of birds is heat, and if a cure is possible—it must be remembered that some diseases are quite incurable—a high temperature will help to get the bird into that state where it will start to feed again. The temperature must be really high to be useful, and anything from 85° to 90°F. is the lowest range that can be considered satisfactory. If the bird is put in a lower temperature, one might just as well save oneself the trouble of producing artificial heat at all.

The best way of providing a bird with a space temperature of this order is to place it in a hospital cage. There can be no doubt whatever that one of the most valuable pieces of equipment that any bird-fancier can ever have is a hospital cage, for it is an investment which will repay its cost many times over a period of a few years.

The idea of the hospital cage is perfectly simple. It is usually a smaller cage than that to which the bird is accustomed. It is constructed with a false bottom under which there is some means of heating, usually electric light bulbs, but in case of need an oil heater will do.

The heat in the hospital cage must be controlled by a thermostat, and these instruments are so accurate today that it is possible to maintain the temperature in a hospital cage to within 2° or 3°F. of what is considered to be the best temperature for effecting a cure. During illness a constant temperature, as well as a high one, is important.

There may be some fanciers capable of constructing their own hospital cages, and in books and periodicals there have been descriptions from time to time giving details as to how these cages can be made, but for the average fancier it is better to purchase one ready-made. Often it is discovered that the cost of materials—not even counting the cost of tools that might have to be purchased if the job is to be undertaken—is greater than the cost of purchasing a ready-made unit.

DISEASES OF THE LIVER

Some birds suffer from liver disease. This trouble may

be caused by unsatisfactory feeding or may result from the fact that the birds have been too closely confined. Usually it does not appear in young birds, but is comparatively common in birds which have been kept in captivity for a number of years. However, most liver troubles can be avoided if the foods provided are very carefully rationed in relation to the bird's age and the exercise it is known to take.

If the birds are allowed an abundance of exercise, and if they belong to species which are active, liver trouble is not likely to cause serious anxiety at any time except perhaps with the odd bird which happens to be abnormal.

DIARRHOEA

Diarrhoea is not a disease in itself, but is usually the symptom of some other minor ailment, or it may, in fact, be an indication of serious disease.

It is very difficult with birds to diagnose any specific disease from diarrhoea itself, because if one is to be really well informed, it is essential that the droppings should be taken away for microscopic investigation. This will show whether there is a bacterial infection, or it may show that there were other causes producing this symptom. By the time such examinations have been carried out very fully, and rarely are they so simple that one microscopic slide will provide the answer to the problem, the bird, if suffering from some serious disease, is probably dead. If it was only an indication of a slight intestinal upset, recovery will already have taken place.

Some birds, however, do suffer from coccidiosis, and it is probable that many birds in the wild are the victims of this disease. If they are young, they die: if they are old, it seems to have very little effect upon them, but it is these old birds, when they are the hosts of coccidia, which are naturally extremely dangerous to young birds with whom they may come into close contact.

CONSTIPATION

Among birds bowel disorders are not at all uncommon, but they are usually the result of incorrect feeding, or they may be the outward sign of an internal chill. If a bird is apparently fit, and yet has difficulty in evacuating itself, this may be an indication that the type of food given has not been sufficiently balanced to produce a normal bowel motion. Frequently a very simple cure in such cases is the provision of extra green food if the birds will eat it. On the other hand, seed which has been treated with a non-toxic mineral oil such as medicinal paraffin will help to improve this condition. It is a surprising fact perhaps, but very rarely do birds which eat seed treated with cod-liver oil suffer from constipation unless the cause of that constipation is something really serious.

It might be wise to state here that all diseases in birds should be regarded as infectious until one has proved that the contrary is, in fact, the truth. Very often the proof is that the other birds do not develop the same disease, but the havoc which some infectious diseases may cause in a collection of birds is so serious that no bird-owner can ever afford to take the slightest risk.

RESPIRATORY DISEASES
Respiratory diseases can be divided into several groups. Birds which are kept in damp, draughty quarters are almost certain to develop chills. A chill, which is something about which humans know quite a lot, can be cured very simply by placing the bird in heat. When it shows signs of recovery, it must be gradually accustomed to the lower temperatures which it will experience in either the cage or the aviary. If pneumonia follows, this is usually accompanied by noisy and difficult breathing. Pneumonia is much more difficult to cure than an ordinary chill, but here again a high temperature is the thing likely to help the bird to resist further complications, and to assist it to overcome the original bacterial infection.

Dusty seed can cause what is apparently a respiratory disease, but if fresh seed which has been thoroughly cleaned is supplied straight away when one has realized what the cause of the trouble may have been, improvement in the condition of the bird will follow very rapidly.

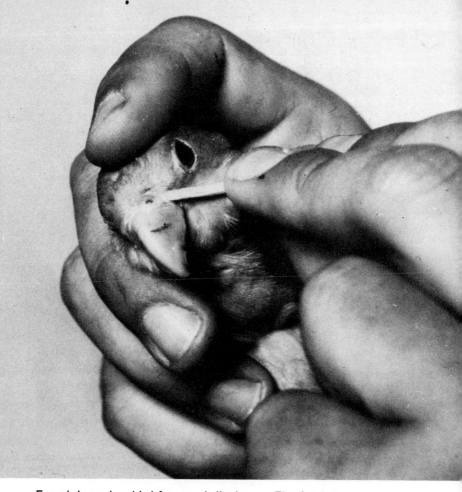

Examining a lovebird for nasal discharge. The feathers around the nostrils are gently peeled back with the aid of a blunt toothpick. Photo by Miceli Studios.

Birds that gasp for air, as if suffering from asthma, may appear in the flock. This is a very contagious ailment and the ill bird should be segregated for some while, even after the symptoms have passed. Recently a specific medicine for respiratory diseases in birds has been placed on the market by Mardel Laboratories. It is Ornacyn and can be obtained in most pet shops.

DISEASES OF THE EYE

It is not at all unusual for birds to be imported into this country with inflamed eyelids, but it is by no means easy to diagnose what is the real cause of this eye trouble. Some diseases of the eye are incurable, but when a bird is noticed with eyes which are red around the lids and the eyeballs are also inflamed, with perhaps some discharge from the eye, then immediately treatment must be started.

Perhaps one of the safest things to use is thiazamide ointment. This contains one of the sulpha drugs and has been known to produce remarkable cures. Golden eye ointment has also been proved to be of great value in such cases.

There are two sorts of conjunctivitis to which birds are subject. One of them clears up very quickly, but the other seems to be so infectious that no sooner does the bird show some sign of improvement than it immediately re-infects itself. This second form usually has to be regarded as incurable.

If eye troubles cannot be cleared up in the space of a fortnight or so, it may be safer to destroy the bird painlessly to prevent the spread of the disease among other birds with which this bird may later come in contact. However, before destroying a bird which may have a sentimental value apart from its monetary value, it will do no harm to consult a vet.

ACCIDENTS

The first of these to be considered is overgrown claws which is, in fact, an accident of Nature.

OVERGROWN CLAWS

Birds which are accustomed in the wild to spend some time on the ground, if they are confined to a cage, may not find suitable conditions for walking. The result of this unnatural environment may be that the claws tend to become too long. The right type of perch often prevents claws from growing too long, whereas the wrong type will tend to allow excessive growth. The cause, however, and its prevention are two entirely different things. What the bird-owner has to do

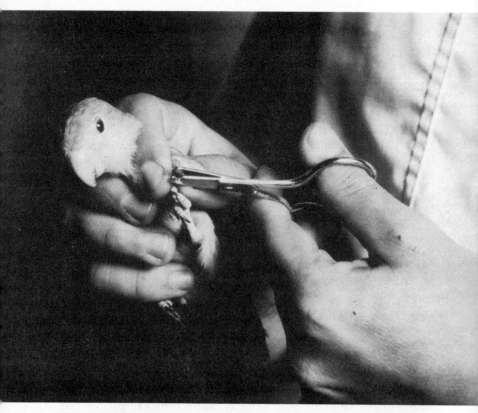

With the bird safely immobilized, the claws can be trimmed. Using a pair of the blunt-tipped scissors designed for the job (special bird-claw scissors available at pet shops have indentations near the tip to allow the claw to fall naturally into a good position for clipping), the tip of the claw can be trimmed back without danger of cutting into the vein. Photo by Miceli Studios.

is to deal with overgrown claws which his bird has developed.

The catching of birds is not easy, but a little skill will allow the owner to catch any bird without frightening it unduly. In an aviary, if the birds are in the flight, a net is often of great value. In a cage it is probably far better to use one's hand and to grasp the bird gently but firmly, and then, holding out each leg separately, to snip off the excessive growth of each claw with a sharp pair of nail clippers. Care has to be taken when performing this minor operation because there is a vein which runs down into the claw, although it does not reach right to the tip. By holding the claw up to the light, this small red vein can be seen easily, and the cutting can be carried out so that it is avoided. When this precaution is taken, there will be no bleeding.

OVERGROWN BEAK

There are birds which are inclined to show excessive growth of the beak, particularly of the upper mandible. When this occurs and the growth is allowed to continue unchecked, it may be extremely difficult in time for the bird to feed. The same method is adopted as with overgrown claws, but for cutting back a beak it is probably safer to use a very sharp pair of scissors. There will be little chance of doing any damage if the upper mandible is cut back so that it fits quite neatly over the lower mandible. It is only very rarely that the lower mandible overgrows, although this does occasionally occur. The trouble can often be prevented by putting in the cage a hard piece of rock or stone against which the bird will frequently strop its beak to clean it, and in this way may prevent the mandible from growing excessively. However, it must not be supposed that this is always a remedy because there are some birds, particularly when they are getting old, which show this overgrowing of the mandibles merely as one of the indications of old age.

EGG-BINDING

Probably there is no bird-keeper with any considerable experience of breeding who has been fortunate enough to avoid egg-binding in his hens. Usually it is not a very serious trouble, but it is most important that the condition should be dealt with immediately or the bird may die.

There are two ways of dealing with this problem. One is by inserting warmed salad oil into the oviduct by means of a small syringe, but this is a remedy which is extremely difficult to employ with very small birds. The other, and far more satisfactory method, is to place the bird in a hospital cage and to raise the temperature to 85°F. Normally, under these circumstances, the egg will be found broken at the bottom of the cage in the course of a few hours. Nothing which is taken into the digestive tract can possibly reach the source of the trouble.

The cause of egg-binding may be that the egg itself is badly formed, or it may be that the shell has not been deposited on the membrane enclosing the white and the yolk. Soft-shelled eggs are always difficult to expel. On the other hand, lack of exercise often results in loss of muscle tone, and if hens try to breed too early in the season, when they have been unable to take adequate exercise, this loss of muscular tone may prevent the hen from laying her first egg easily. Whatever happens, when the egg has been removed, the hen should not be allowed to lay again for several weeks. She should be separated from the cock and rested so that she can recover from the strain of the ordeal she has undergone. By that time her general condition too will probably be much better, and she will have no trouble with a further clutch of eggs.

FRACTURES

Birds suffer accident from time to time, usually as the result of a fright, for when they are alarmed they dash about in a most unintelligent fashion, and in this state can easily break either a wing or a leg. A broken wing is very difficult to treat, and probably it is better to leave it completely alone. If, however, the wing is hanging down, the broken bone may join if adhesive strapping is used to hold the wing in position. Splinting is quite impossible. Most normal wing breaks are slight, and the muscles of the wing will hold the bones in position, but it is most unlikely that any fracture of a bone in the wing will heal in such a way that the wing will ever be absolutely normal again.

Broken legs are much more easily dealt with, and even the smallest birds can be splinted. For small birds, match-sticks, which are bound round the leg with adhesive plaster, will very often produce a join which is only distinguishable afterwards by a slight thickening of the leg where the fracture actually occured. Compound fractures of the leg usually mean amputation.

Patience is of inestimable value in dealing with fractures, and deft fingers are essential. Usually to splint a leg requires the efforts of two people, but there is great satisfaction in being able to get a bird back on to two feet when the alternative was probably the loss of a limb.

PARASITES

Parasites cannot strictly be regarded as either disease or accident, but they are often a cause of disease, and every effort should be made to see that birds are kept entirely free from all forms of parasites.

Once parasites begin to multiply they can be more than just a nuisance—they can be fatal, leading to severe debilitation and disease transmittal. Prevention through cleanliness of cages and proper use of pesticidal agents is the key to coping with a potential parasite problem. Photo by Miceli Studios.

Occasionally birds are found to be infested with worms, but when that is the case, they have usually been imported with them and die within a comparatively short space of time.

Red mite, however, is an entirely different problem.

Red mite, which is the bugbear of the fancier who keeps his birds in cages, is something which can be cured, but the great thing is to prevent these pests from finding suitable hiding places. There are perches available with mite traps at the end which help to keep the pest at bay, and also to allow the birdkeeper to deal adequately with any colonies of these most objectionable little creatures. One of the best things to do is to take the perches out of infected cages and to immerse them in paraffin for some time. After that they must be thoroughly scrubbed and dried before they are put into use again.

The place where most red mites collect is always at the end of the perches, but the corners and inside edges of the edges of the cage should also receive attention. A cage which is known to be infested should be taken out of use and dealt with very adequately before birds are put in it again. Red mites only live on the birds at night, so if a bird is taken out of a cage during the day and put into a cage known to be clean, the chances are that this bird will have no further trouble.

This is really a very short section to cover what is obviously an extremely wide subject, but experience has shown that apart from the curing of minor ills there is really very little that the bird-fancier can do except to make use of the hospital cage. Those small birds which are usually kept in cages as pets have such a slender hold on life, even at the best of times, that in the case of serious illness the space of time between life and death may often be only a matter of hours.

7: LOVEBIRDS

There are very many parrots and parrot-like birds in the world, but few of them are readily obtainable, and most that can be bought today are expensive. There is, however, one group of birds, some of the members of which can be obtained comparatively easily, and two or three species which are, in fact, quite common. They are the lovebirds which will be the only group of parrot-like birds to be considered in this book.

They are all species which come from Africa, and three of them are common despite the present limitations on the importation of parrot-like birds.

Lovebirds are difficult to sex, with the exception of one species, but this is a minor detail, and no one who knows them will deny their great attractiveness. Practically all of them have been bred in captivity, some of them with comparative ease.

Feeding is quite simple. A seed mixture composed of canary, white millet and small yellow millet is their basic diet, and to this should be added a number of extras. Sunflower seed, hemp and rape can also be used; sunflower quite generously, but hemp and rape with a good deal of discretion, with just a few of these seeds daily for each bird, but no more. This seed diet should also be supplemented by green food. They are very fond of all green foods, and have no particular fads or fancies. Chickweed, dandelion leaf, lettuce and spinach are all readily accepted, and seeding grasses are a delight to them whenever these are available. Of such seeding grasses probably rye is their first favorite, and should be given to them as often as possible.

Insectile mixtures and insects themselves do not interest them at all. Even when they are provided, the birds will not look at them. There is something that the owner can do, and that is to sprout seeds during the winter when green food is not so easily come by and seeding grasses are impossible to obtain.

On the whole, lovebirds are healthy birds and rarely ail in captivity if treated with common sense. They will live for a number of years, and most species will breed, but only two of them can be regarded as really free breeders.

Some species are more popular than others, probably because they are more easily available, and in the following section they are dealt with in the order of their availability.

PEACH-FACED LOVEBIRD (*Agapornis roseicollis*)

This species, which is found chiefly in South-west Africa, is sometimes called the Rosy-face Lovebird, but the more common name is the Peach-faced. It is without doubt among the most beautiful of all the lovebirds which have ever been imported. It has been bred with great success in North America and is probably more numerous than all the other species of lovebirds combined.

None of the lovebirds is really peaceful, but perhaps the most spiteful of the whole genus is the Peach-faced. It is most unwise ever to keep more than one pair together in the same aviary. They never seem to get on well with other birds either of the same size or even with those which are larger. When two pairs are put together there will be constant bickering; a good deal of damage will certainly be done to the feathers. It is quite likely that as a result of their constant quarreling there will be some toes missing at the end of the season, and to add to the dismal story there will be no satisfactory breeding results to record.

Sometimes even a true pair get on badly together when they are not breeding, but it is rather surprising that two hens, or even two cocks, will sometimes settle down reasonably happily together and spend very little time quarrelling.

Like several other species of lovebirds, the Peach-faced carries its nesting material to the box by tucking the stripped-off bark in its rump and under the feathers of the back. It often carries a considerable quantity of material in this way as a prelude to the construction of a fairly large but carelessly built nest.

For a pair of Peach-faced Lovebirds, a box of ample proportions is necessary. It is a common practice for both the cock and the hen to spend the night together in the same box, even when the hen is busy with the incubating of the eggs. As the fancier will soon learn, Peach-faced Lovebirds always prefer to roost in a box rather than to sleep on a perch. This is not a serious disadvantage, because generally they are not such free breeders that they will be prepared to breed all the year round. It is not unusual for them to moult late in the year, and that at once puts an end to all desire for breeding. When they do moult at this time, the nest-box can safely be kept in the shelter, and there will be little likelihood of their making any attempt to breed.

The number of eggs laid is usually four, but occasionally as many as six will be found in the nest. It is the hen who does most of the incubating, although, as has already been stated, the cock likes to share the box with her, particularly at night. It is doubtful, however, whether he spends any time on the eggs at all. A most interesting fact is that even if the cock has been somewhat quarrelsome before nesting has started, he is a most attentive husband while the hen is setting and will feed her many times a day as she sits in the box. His devotion is so contrary to his normal behavior that it becomes amusing.

Determining the sex of Peach-face Lovebirds is difficult. All that is possible to do is to put a pair together hopefully and then to wait to see what happens. As a rule hens get on better together than cocks, and if two birds are extremely peaceful, the possibility is that two hens are living together.

Cocks, too, usually take only a small part in the building of the nest—some cocks take no part at all—and thus, any bird which is seen stripping the bark off either willow or any other branch such as hazel or lime is more likely than not a hen. Even this test is not decisive. One may be compelled to try several birds together before a true pair has been obtained.

The head of the Peach-faced Lovebird is a really bright red, and the forepart is a particularly bright shade of rose. The color on the cheeks is paler and is a distinct pink of the same color as that found on the throat and breast. The pink of the breast, however, shows a very distinct tinge of yellow which creates the impression of the color of a peach, from which fact the bird has derived its name.

Green is the color along the back, but it is of a darker shade than is usually found on the Red-faced Lovebird, to which it is very similar in general appearance. On the rump there is a bright blue patch, but the tail is more of a blue-green, clearly barred with black. When the tail is spread out fanwise, it is possible to see very distinct markings of orange-red which make a brave show of color, but the upper tail coverts are a distinct blue without other markings.

While the wings are almost of the same shade as the back, they also show some signs of black. The lower part of the breast and the belly are a distinct green, definitely yellow in tone on the breast, but without the same brightness of color on the belly and under the vent.

FISCHER'S LOVEBIRD (*Agapornis fischeri*)

Fischer's Lovebird is easily obtained if a fancier wishes to make a start with the birds of this group.

This species was first imported in 1926 and comes from the Victoria Nyanza area of Africa. When Fischer's Love-birds were first imported, they were never found difficult to acclimatize but now the problem of acclimatization does not arise, because those birds which one is able to buy have been bred in this country. Aviary-bred stock certainly has to get used to its new surrounding when it passes from one fancier to another, but this is not acclimatization.

Some bird-lovers have tried to keep Fischer's Lovebird in a cage, but these birds are not at all suited to cage life. For some reason they seem to be very unhappy when closely confined, and in a cage they sometimes moult continuously. So unhappy are they that they often get down on to the floor of the cage and hide their heads in the corner as though they have no further interest life. Another point that one notices when they are kept in a cage is that they are inclined to become too fat, and when this happens the length of their life is considerably reduced. Thus, they ought to be regarded as essentially aviary birds.

They are reasonably hardy and do not seem to mind cold weather, although they should be protected from cold winds during the winter. Some fanciers have felt that the best thing to do was to cage them during the cold weather, and then bring them into the house, but this is not a policy to be recommended, for the simple reason that they are so unhappy under these conditions, and are most likely to be unfit for breeding early the next year if they are treated in this way. When they are kept outdoors and allowed to stay in a shelter from which the nest-box has been removed, it is more than probable that early in the next season they will get to work to produce a family, but it is not wise to allow them to start too early.

As lovebirds go they are not particularly spiteful, but none of the species in this group is really safe with small birds, and it is perhaps better to give them a fair-sized aviary all to themselves. It is a remarkable thing, but a fact which has been noticed on a number of occasions, that two pairs of Fischer's Lovebirds get on quite happily together without any quarrelling, although they will not tolerate the close proximity of any other species of lovebird.

These are very pretty little birds, not much more than 5 in. in length. In outward appearance there is no difference at all between the sexes. Sometimes one can distinguish between the cock and hen of some particular species, even when the colors are very much alike, because of the brighter general coloring of the cock. This is certainly not the case with Fischer's Lovebird, for, surprisingly, one sometimes notices that it is the hen that is brighter than the cock. The only way in which it is possible to distinguish sex is by behavior, and even that method presents a number of problems from time to time.

If you have two cocks together, it is most unlikely that either of them will go into the nest-box, but, if you have two hens, they will certainly go into the nest. From this rather exasperating fact one comes to realize that it is only by careful observation and deduction that the sexes can be ultimately distinguished.

A large number of eggs, with none of them fertile, points almost certainly to two hens, while two birds which make no attempt to go to nest at all are probably two cocks. It is just possible that a cock might start to build a nest, but if this bird got no further than the preliminaries, the problem of sex would still be far from being solved.

The easiest way of dealing with the problem is to buy a pair of birds which have been sexed already because they have actually bred. A true pair that has produced and reared a family is a good investment if one can also be assured that the birds are not old.

The general color is green, rather darker on the nape and shoulders than along the back, but still, even there, of a bright green shade. The tint on the nape and shoulders is olive, whereas on the back it is much more a darker grass-green. On the underside the color is paler even, as there is a definite hint of yellow on the green. Just at the rump the color is a very bright but dark shade of blue, while the feathers of the tail are green, although tipped with blue of a slightly lighter shade than that which is found on the rump.

Right across the front of the head, on the forehead, is a distinct band of orange-red. It is, in fact, more orange than red. The cheeks are also orange, but are considerably paler than the band on the head, whereas on the throat this orange loses its redness and becomes yellow, but is also slightly tinged with pink.

Round the eye is a distinctive white ring which gives the birds a rather amusing appearance.

The beak is red and its shade is often a clear indication of the condition of the bird. Careful observation will usually show that birds which are in really first-class breeding condition have beaks which are a darker red then than at any other time.

Fischer's Lovebird will breed all the year round, although, of course, to allow it to do so would be courting disaster, for young birds produced from parents which have been allowed to breed too freely are usually lacking in stamina. Such stock is useless to any fancier.

For breeding a nest-box is required. One which is an 8-in. cube is satisfactory for the purpose, and the entrance hole should not be less than 2 in. in diameter. Rather remarkably lovebirds, unlike most species which belong to the parrot family, do actually build a nest. These nests are very crude in construction, but nevertheless, for satisfactory breeding, the birds must be given an opportunity to produce what to them at least is a satisfactory home for the young. For this purpose they should be given fresh twigs. Hazel is probably preferred to all others, but if it is not available, small branches of other non-poisonous trees are almost equally good and will be accepted. What the birds do is to strip the bark from these small branches, and from these strips construct a very rough nest.

It is almost impossible to say how many eggs will be laid, although there has seemed to be a tendency over the past few years for the number of eggs in a clutch to increase on average. However, six may be regarded as a normal clutch.

The period of incubation is ten days, and the moment when the first chick hatches is obvious, for the parents start to feed at once. Fischer's Lovebirds are careful feeders, although sometimes they are not very successful and the young seem to die of starvation. The reason for this is difficult to explain or even understand. It may be that the fact that now this species is producing more young than was the case formerly means that the quality of food provided by the parents for their young is unsatisfactory because it is lacking in certain essentials such as the right amount of protein. Another result of bad feeding is that it is not at all unusual to get young birds coming out of the nest badly feathered and also not too well developed physically. Certainly these young, when they do eventually emerge from the nest, are poor, helpless little creatures, and unless considerable care is taken to see that they are protected from the weather, particularly rain and wind, they are more likely to die than to survive. Young birds which are weak should be placed in some small receptacle from which they are unable to escape, but where the parents can get to them and feed them easily. The fancier can also help by hand-feeding several times a day.

The young, when fully feathered, are very similar in appearance to adults, but there is not the same difference in the tones of green; in fact, the head, neck and sides, and also the back, are much more of an olive shade all over than is the case with adults. There is also a difference in the shade of orange both on the forehead, cheeks and throat. It is definitely paler in young birds than in adults.

All lovebirds are fascinating creatures, but Fischer's Lovebird is probably among the most fascinating of all, and it is the species that many beginners form a lasting attachment to even though other species are kept.

It is not a very musical bird, but the noise it makes is not unpleasant, and in an aviary it is very attractively active and its antics are always amusing, for it is an acrobat of no mean ability.

Feeding calls for no special comment here, as all the lovebirds can be fed in more or less the same way. Not all of them show the same inclination to eat the same foods on any particular day, but if they are given a fairly wide choice they will get on quite happily and will thrive.

Some of the supplementary foods rich in protein, which have recently been provided for the breeder of budgerigars, may also be found useful as an addition to the diet of lovebirds and Fischer's in particular.

MASKED LOVEBIRD (*Agapornis personata*)

The Masked certainly has one really great advantage in that it is a good breeder, and there is a strong possibility that there will be no difficulty in the future in obtaining the Masked Lovebird as a result of the considerable numbers which will be bred by fanciers in this country.

It was first introduced into Britain in 1926 and was imported from the Tanzania area of Africa.

Not all lovebirds are absolutely hardy, and few of them can really endure the most rigorous winters without any protection at all, but the Masked Lovebird can certainly tolerate temperatures in the region of the freezing-point without coming to any harm. Winter is not the time of year, of course, during which to allow any lovebird species to breed, because, if breeding is attempted in very cold weather, egg-binding is almost certain to follow.

With some breeders the Masked has earned a reputation for being a spiteful bird, but this reputation is not entirely deserved by the species as a whole. There are birds of this species which are extremely spiteful and dangerous to other birds, and very often it is actually the hens which show considerably more ill-feeling than any cock. If a fancier is unlucky enough to get hold of a pair of birds which display this unpleasant characteristic, he will probably find that unless the aviary is large the pair will also quarrel a good deal among themselves and will be absolutely unsafe with any other birds, even those as large as a budgerigar. Despite the existence of such really vicious pairs, it would be unfair to assume that all Masked Lovebirds are spiteful; some of them get on perfectly happily together. They can be quiet and peaceful birds and, even if they are not always kindly disposed towards other species, they do get on well together and set about the business of breeding readily. To put two pairs of Masked Lovebirds in the same aviary, however, is asking for trouble.

The length of this species is roughly 6 in., and if either bird appears larger than the other, it is more often than not the hen which shows a slightly greater length of body.

Like most lovebirds, the Masked builds a nest and is more careful than some of the other birds belonging to this genus in the way in which it builds the home for its future family. It strips the bark from the branches with great precision and, although no one could suggest that the nest was carefully woven, it is indeed a tidy structure. The best place for the nest-box is out in the flight where the damp of the atmosphere will prevent the inside from becoming too dry. It is a good plan to protect the lid of the box by covering the flight just above it, but the sides can safely be allowed to become wet with the rain which is bound to be driven in by the wind. In fact, moisture is essential for successful hatching. But that does not mean that the breeder should try to add this moisture himself! If he does, the chances are that his success will be considerably less than if he had left matters to Nature. When there is insufficient humidity in the nest-box, there are certain to be dead-in-shell chicks.

Both birds take a hand in building the nest and are more selective than some species in the type of material they choose. Hazel will be accepted readily, but if there is a choice between hazel and willow, willow will always be the first to be picked up, probably because it is much easier to strip than most other woods. The bark of this tree is very pliable when it has been stripped, and has another great virtue in that it retains its moisture for a considerable period, certainly for the length of time that the eggs will be in the box.

The number of eggs laid may be four or five, but early in the season it is not uncommon for some, if not all, of these eggs to be clear. This fact in itself is sufficient argument for not allowing the birds to make a start too early.

Once a pair of Masked Lovebirds decides to breed, they are prepared to continue the business all the year round, but every attempt must be made to prevent them from breeding during the winter months. They may be allowed to use the nest-box, but if they are supplied with no nesting material and there is only an empty box, the chances are that the hen will not attempt to lay. If she does, it may be necessary to remove the nest-box altogether.

The color of the head of this species is usually black, but sometimes the shade varies quite considerably, and the forehead may even be a dark brown. Occasionally one comes across a bird which will undoubtedly be a male, on which the head is dark brown all over, although in normal lighting it appears to be almost black when seen from a distance.

This species also carries an eye circle which is wide and very clearly defined.

The brown of the head ends at the back of the crown, and from there the neck and nape are a very bright yellow, while the top of the back also shows the same color, but perhaps of a slightly more golden shade. It is the throat that shows the brightest yellow area, and on some birds this may even be distinctly orange with more than a hint of red in it. The breast is of a paler yellow shade than that on the top of the back. From the mantle, the rest of the back along to the rump is green, but the rump itself is actually blue. This blue is a dark shade which is most attractive, but it is never particularly bright in tone.

On the underside the yellow of the breast is sharply cut off to become a yellow-green, a color which is carried through on to the belly and then right under the vent. The wings are also green.

The green of the tail is slightly darker than that on the back and is also different in appearance because of black markings in the feathers. The beak is red.

Once a pair of birds have settled down to nesting, even if they have been inclined to be quarrelsome before, that state of mind quickly disappears, and the cock is always most anxious to take some share in the incubating of the eggs. He does not sit as frequently or for such long periods as the hen, but he does take his turn, and becomes extremely fussy (but also very helpful) when the chicks eventually hatch.

BLUE-MASKED LOVEBIRD

The bird discussed immediately above is often called the Black-masked Lovebird because it is a Lovebird that has a black mask. That is good logic. But the most common mutation of that species is called the Blue-masked Lovebird and that is very confusing because it does not have a blue mask.

The Blue-masked Lovebird first appeared in a California aviary in the 1930's. It had blue feathers where the normal had green, and white feathers where the normal had yellow. The mask was unchanged.

Now well established, this variety is available at reasonable prices. It breeds well in aviary or large cage and makes a most satisfactory variety for the beginner.

In recent years other mutant forms of the Masked Lovebird have appeared, including cinnamon, pied, white, and lutino (buttercup yellow).

NYASALAND LOVEBIRD (*Agapornis lilianae*)

It is in many ways remarkable that the Nyasaland Lovebird should be so extremely rare in captivity, as it has the reputation of being a free breeder. It is probable that although there have been many reports of breeding successes, for some reason these young may not have carried through until the next season when they would be adult. It is also quite certain that infertility is, and always has been, a characteristic of the Nyasaland Lovebird. A lutino (buttercup yellow) mutation is now well established.

The number of eggs laid varies from two to as many as seven. Judging from the reports of those who have kept this species over a long period of years, practically all clutches contain a percentage of clear eggs which is rarely less than a third.

At the present time it would be extremely difficult for the would-be owner of the Nyasaland to obtain a pair. If he reads those advertisements in the press dealing with foreign birds, it will be a real occasion if he ever sees a pair offered for sale.

As the name implies, this bird comes from Malawi, previously called Nyasaland, but its distribution is somewhat wider, for it is also found in Rhodesia.

It is a small bird, probably the smallest of the lovebirds, for it rarely exceeds 4¼ in. in length. There is no real difference in the sexes, and it is always extremely difficult to pick a pair even should enough birds be available for such a choice to be attempted. It has been said that the hen is flatter in skull than the cock, but this must be regarded as a very uncertain guide. The only safe way would be to judge sex by behavior.

When it comes to breeding, it is usually the Nyasaland cock who is the first to make a move, and his interest in the nest and in his partner is often an indication that he is a cock. On the other hand, if two hens are together, there may no interest in the nest-box at all except as a roosting-place.

Most of the lovebirds build a nest from the stripped bark of hazel, lime, elk, or willow. The Nyasaland not only uses such tree bark but also some of the actual twigs themselves.

The front of the head and cheeks and throat are orange, but the darkest shade of this color is found on the forehead. Where the orange of the head finishes, the color becomes a distinct yellow, but this turns to green on the nape and this is the color which is carried right along the back of the bird. It is a bright green, very similar to that of young grass, but is darker than the green which is shown on the breast, for there the color is made even lighter by the addition of yellow. The beak is red.

ABYSSINIAN LOVEBIRD (*Agapornis taranta*]

The Abyssinian Lovebird has been known for a considerable time. During recent years, however, it has been very scarce indeed and difficult to obtain.

It has been bred in captivity on a number of occasions but it could not be considered a free breeder. It is perhaps for this reason that comparatively few fanciers who are interested in lovebirds have troubled about it.

One decided advantage which it has over several of the other species is that it is hardy, well above the average, and does not seem to be put out in the least by wide ranges of temperature. This does not mean that it should be subjected to the rigors of a severe winter, for practically all lovebirds are better if they are sheltered and provided with some artificial heat during this period.

The Abyssinian is slightly larger than the other species of the genus, and it is not unusual for some specimens to exceed 6½ in. in length. Perhaps in some ways it is not as elegant as the others, because it seems to be a little more thick-set, and it is definitely not as attractive to the eye. In fact, it has almost a forbidding appearance, and this may possibly be another reason why it has never become popular. This appearance in no way belies its true character, for it is a bird which never becomes really friendly, and the fancier who has kept a pair for a considerable time may still find it most difficult to handle. It will peck not only at other birds, but also at anybody who handles it. Strangely enough, when it pecks in this fashion it does not seem to be the result of fear, but actually that it is just spiteful, which compels one to regard it as being a bird of rather unpleasant character.

Its general color pattern is not very prepossessing either, for this species is practically green all over. Actually, there are a number of different shades of green to be seen on the feathers, but there is no brightness of color such as one always sees in the Masked or the Peach-faced Lovebirds. The head is dark green, but in the male, across the front of the forehead and extending slightly higher on the head, is a red band which is not found on the hen. Thus, in adult birds this color difference is a deciding factor in sexing.

On the neck and nape the shade of green is considerably darker than on the top of the head and along the back, and is often quite a dusky green with a tendency towards a brownish shade. Round the eye there are a number of red feathers which are a rather remarkable feature of this species. The color on the underside is also green, but is definitely paler than on top. On the wings the green is of a deep shade showing some traces of black. This wing color is very similar to the tail, which is also green but is actually barred with black. The beak is red.

As there are so few Abyssinian Lovebirds in captivity today, it is not surprising that reports of their breeding activities are comparatively uncommon.

RED-FACED LOVEBIRD (*Agapornis pullaria*)

It is rather surprising that success has never been achieved with this species because, as with all foreign birds, breeding success depends very largely on providing the right environment, and it is amazing that this bird should seem to need something so different from closely related species. It has been suggested that the Red-faced Lovebird actually breeds by burrowing into the ant-hills of the white ant, and there, at the end of a long tunnel, it makes a hollow in which to lay its eggs. Breeders have tried to produce artificial anthills to give the Red-faced Lovebird an opportunity of burrowing this tunnel for itself, and it has sometimes happened that a tunnel has actually been made, but after this great effort the birds have shown no further interest in the tunnel and eggs have not been laid.

One of the greatest attractions of the Red-faced Lovebird is its constant activity. It is never entirely happy in a cage and, like so many birds of this genus, when confined too closely, spends a lot of its time on the floor and seems to take little or no interest in what is going on around it. But if you put it outside in an aviary where it has plenty of space, it is full of life and flies about happily from perch to perch almost all day long.

Exceptional pairs will live quite contentedly in a cage, but they are very unusual and certainly not typical of the species. These birds soon become bored unless they are given plenty at which they can peck. The fancier should provide them with pieces of wood, with the bark on, suspended from the wall of the cage, or they will in time become so bored that they will peck each other. There seems to be little spitefulness in this behavior, but they do the job so thoroughly that they completely ruin the appearance of the plumage of any companion.

With other birds the Red-faced Lovebird is inclined to mind its own business and remain reasonably peaceful, but that does not mean that it can ever be trusted with birds considerably smaller than itself. In fact, it is never safe to put any lovebirds in with small finches, and to put them with waxbills can have only one inevitable consequence.

On the whole the Red-faced Lovebird is less colorful than most of the other lovebirds, but, as its name implies, it has a red face. The top of the head and the forehead are a very bright red, but down on the cheeks and throat the color is several shades paler. Although the beak is also red, there is a distinct hint of orange in this color.

Just behind the crown the color is green with a tinge of yellow about it, but the shade gradually becomes darker on the nape and along the back where it may be almost as dark as myrtle green. The wings are slightly paler than the back, but the breast is a very distinct yellow-green and of very pleasant appearance.

As in the case of the Masked Lovebird, there is a very definite patch of blue on the rump which is a little paler in shade on the Red-faced than on the Masked Lovebird.

The tail is also green and shows a number of different shades, not only on the feathers as a whole but also on the same feather. Some feathers are a dark and almost dull green down the shaft, but yellow-green on the outer edges of the web.

On the underside the yellow-green of the breast gradually becomes darker as it approaches the belly, and it is a really deep shade of green under the vent.

The inexperienced fancier always finds it extremely difficult to distinguish the sexes, but on the whole it will be found that the hen has a paler face and that the red areas on her body are less in size than on the cock. If this were the only guide to sex, however, it would soon prove to be most unreliable, and as is so often the case, the fancier is compelled ultimately to rely very largely upon behavior to help him to make up his mind which bird is, in fact, the cock and which the hen.

It has been said that the under-wing coverts of the cock are black, but although some cocks do show black feathers in this area, as a guide to sex that too must be regarded as unreliable.

The Red-faced Lovebird is not among the most hardy of the group, and when first imported requires a good deal of care. It is always sound practice to take a freshly imported pair and to confine them to a large cage until they have become acclimatized. During that time the birds' feathers may suffer considerably from their unfortunate habit of climbing about on the bars of the cage, but as a precaution, cage life for some weeks, and certainly until spring has come, is definitely advisable. Even when they have spent a summer and autumn outside, they must till be protected during the winter, for they cannot stand either cold or draught. They may be kept in an outside aviary which has a suitably protected shelter, but even there they will thrive better if the temperature is kept above 40° F.

BLACK-CHEEKED LOVEBIRD (*Agapornis nigrigensis*)

Any fancier who wishes to buy a pair of these birds may have to wait a very long time before he finds them. That this should be the case is a great pity, because perhaps of all the birds of this genus, the Black-cheeked is the most friendly. This statement must not be taken to imply that it is a safe bird in a mixed collection, for it would indeed be an exaggeration when made with reference to any species of lovebird. The Black-cheeked species is, nevertheless, much more manageable when handled by its owner. With patience it will in time become reasonably tame.

In many respects it is similar in appearance to the Masked Lovebird, but there is no real difficulty in separating the two species when they can be seen side by side. When either of these species is adult, the Black-cheeked is definitely smaller, and the color of its mask, and also the extent of this mask, is very different from that of the Masked Lovebird.

Black-cheeked Lovebirds come from northern Rhodesia, and even there, apparently, they are not particularly common. At no time have importations been of any size, although there was a time when a few birds were brought over quite frequently. Sometimes only two or three birds were sent at a time, however.

Those who have kept this species have found it to be not too difficult to breed. Once a true pair has been obtained, the birds usually set to work with some degree of urgency to build a nest and rear a family. As rearers, they are extremely good parents, perhaps better than any of the other lovebirds that have been bred in this country.

In construction the nest is typical. When the eggs are laid the hen does most of the incubation. She may lay as many as six eggs, although it is very rare for all of them to be hatched, for one or two may be clear. Dead-in-shell is another hazard.

A rather remarkable thing about this bird, which is,

generally speaking, less spiteful than other lovebirds, is that there have been reports of the cocks attacking their young before they have become fully independent. The reason for this unnatural behavior may well be that the cock is anxious for the hen to go to nest again. Those who have bred this species in this country have sometimes been compelled to adopt the policy of taking away the young earlier than they would like and, after having done this, finishing off the rearing themselves by hand rather than leaving it to the parents.

The Black-cheeked Lovebird is amongst the most hardy of this group and, when it has become acclimatized, can endure considerable variations in temperature. It does not even seem to be distressed if the thermometer gives a reading below freezing-point. It is, however, wiser to protect the birds by confining them to the shelter during the winter and not to allow them to spend too much time in the open flight.

The front of the head, including the forehead, is a very dark brown, but on the crown this color is much lighter and can reasonably be considered as almost chestnut in color. On the cheeks and throat the shade is very much darker and, although never absolutely black, is a really dark brown very similar to that seen on Masked Lovebirds. However, on the top of the breast the color is most distinctive of the species, for here it is a pink with the addition of orange to produce what is sometimes called salmon.

While the back is green without any trace of yellow, the nape itself is a distinct yellow-green. The underside is similar to the nape in actual base color, but the yellow is perhaps not quite so noticeable. The tail is a medium shade of green without any trace of yellow.

Perhaps of all the lovebirds that have been imported, the Black-cheeked is the one which is most suited to cage life. It never seems to be unhappy when confined, and, if the cage is large enough, it will remain active and keep in good condition over a long period.

It is a pity that this species is so rare, but, as it will breed and may even have as many as three families a year, there is a distinct possibility that in the course of time enough birds will be bred in captivity to make it possible for those who would like to keep this species to buy a pair. The present rarity means that the price is high. It is probable that for some considerable time to come the Black-cheeked Lovebird will be out of the reach of the ordinary fancier whose expenditure on his hobby has to be carefully limited.

MADAGASCAR LOVEBIRD (*Agapornis cana*)

It may seem unnecessary to write about the Madagascar Lovebird because it is so extremely rare. It is in the hope that it will at some time in the future become available that a short description of its appearance and behavior will be given here.

Although it is called the Madagascar Lovebird, it is not confined entirely to that island, but can be found in quite a number of adjacent territories.

It is smaller than many of the lovebirds which have been kept in captivity for it very rarely attains a length greater than 5½ in.

Like so many of the lovebirds it is spiteful, particularly so during the breeding season. A cock and a hen get on so badly together that it is usually wise to keep them apart until it is known that they are ready to breed.

An interesting fact about the Madagascar Lovebird is that when it builds its nest it does something which is very rarely done by any of the other species. It not only uses bark and twigs, but incorporates some leaves in the nest as well.

Those who have kept this species say that it is hardy, but the advice is always given that during the winter it should be protected and confined to a flight cage of considerable size in a draught-proof shelter. It will be certainly none the worst if it is also provided with some artificial heat.

The head of the cock is grey, but there is a very slight hint of blue about this color. It has been referred to as lavender-grey, but probably that implies more blue than usually apparent. The rest of the coloring is green except for the upper breast, where the color is again grey, but in this area there is no blue apparent at all.

On the tail there are black markings, but the general

You will invest both money and affection in any lovebird you purchase, so it is important to start out with healthy stock purchased from a reputable seller. Try to purchase your bird from an established seller who has an investment in his business and therefore good reason to avoid the ill will caused by the sale of birds in bad health. This Black-masked Lovebird is in excellent condition. Photo by Louise Van der Meid.

tone of color is similar to that of the back and of the wings.

A hen can be easily distinguished because she does not show the grey which is characteristic of the cock.

Although the Madagascar Lovebird rarely shows any great desire to breed, if a pair do decide to make a start, they are really efficient at the job. It is the hen who does the sitting. During the time that she incubates the eggs, which is over a period of eighteen days, the cock is most careful in his attentions to her. He sees that her needs are met by constantly feeding her, frequently much more often than she desires.

Index

Page numbers set in **bold** type refer to illustrations.